SHARK ATTACK!

SHARK ATTACK!

Greg Norman's guide to aggressive golf

Greg Norman with George Peper

Pan Books Sydney and Auckland

First published 1987 by
The Macmillan Company of Australia Pty Ltd
This edition published 1988 by
Pan Books (Aust) Pty Ltd
68 Moncur Street, Woollahra, Sydney

9 8 7 6 5 4 3 2 1

Norman, Greg, 1955-
Shark attack!
Includes index.
ISBN 0 330 27117 2.
1. Norman, Greg, 1955- . 2. Golf.
I. Peper, George. II. Title.
796.352'3

Printed in Australia by
Globe Press, Victoria

Contents

ACKNOWLEDGEMENTS

I know how to play aggressive golf, but to write this book about it I needed help. My thanks go to George Peper, the editor of *Golf* magazine, who so capably put my ideas in writing. I'm also grateful for the foreword provided by Jack Nicklaus, whose books were my first references. The instructional photography was done by Leonard Kamsler and the colour by another of the world's top golf photographers, my old friend Lawrence Levy. My thanks also to Paul Jennis for the illustrations. I appreciate the support of my editors, Kyle Cathie of Macmillan and Bob Bender of Simon & Schuster, and the guidance of my business manager, Hughes Norton, and the many others at International Management Group.

GREG NORMAN
Orlando, Florida
September, 1987

To my father and mother, Merv and Toini;

To my wife, Laura;

And especially to my coach, Charlie Earp, for his guidance.

Foreword

The first time I had the pleasure of watching Greg Norman play golf was when we were paired in the 1976 Australian Open in Sydney. Greg was twenty-one years old and coming off his first pro victory. He was something of a sensation in the press that week and I recall that, in his nervousness, he shot an 80 in the first round. The next day young Greg showed some of the determination and character that have made him into one of the best players in the game today when he shot 72. After that round we chatted by our lockers, and I let him know that I believed he had a great future in the game. Greg may not have believed me at the time, but, boy, was I right!

It was only later that I learned that Greg was too shy on that occasion to mention that his first taste of golf instruction had been from my book *Golf My Way*. When I wrote that book, my goal was to give something back to the game by helping young people to become good players and by sharing some of the enjoyment I have received from golf over the years. I never dreamed that one of those young readers would grow up to be a player of Greg's calibre. Needless to say, I'm very pleased.

Of course, there are certain things that no one could ever teach Greg Norman – his courage, his charisma, his determination, and his unparalleled belief in himself. These are some of the qualities that Greg conveys in this book. Beyond imparting the instructional aspects of his superb game, he exhorts his followers to strive for their absolute best just as he has done.

There is no finer gentleman in golf, no more gracious winner or loser than Greg. When I won the 1986 Masters there were several players who had a great shot at winning and who ended up disappointed. But only Greg, perhaps the most disappointed of all, took the trouble to stay around until after the presentation ceremony just to offer his personal congratulations. It meant a lot to me and it says a lot about him. Greg is more than a great player and a great competitor. He's a great friend.

JACK NICKLAUS

CHAPTER 1

Aptitude Starts With Attitude

THE AGGRESSOR'S EDGE

There are several good ways to swing at a golf ball, but only one good way to play golf – aggressively.

Picture the swings of Arnold Palmer, Jack Nicklaus and Seve Ballesteros – three very distinctive styles. Yet each of those players has demonstrated time and again that he knows how to grab hold of a tournament and subdue a course. Each knows how – and when – to be aggressive.

Aggressive play is a vital asset of the world's greatest golfers. However, it's even *more* important to the average player. Attack this game in a bold, confident and determined way, and you'll take the biggest step imaginable towards realising your full potential as a player. You'll also make a giant leap over the heads of your fellow players, because most weekend golfers are anything but aggressive.

I can't tell you how many players I've seen who cripple themselves with a cautious, frightened attitude. It pervades their entire game, beginning with the teeshot. On a tight or difficult driving hole, I can see the fear in their eyes. This fearing attitude leads to a steering swing and a veering teeshot.

On approach shots, they rarely take enough club to go boldly at the flag. Instead they fall short, where most of the architect's worst perils lurk. From bunkers, these players are completely intimidated. As a result, they fail to make the necessary accelerating swing, and either they leave the ball in the sand or blade it across the green into another bunker, leading to even greater trauma on the next shot.

Many amateur golfers are good pitchers and chippers, but they lack the ideal attitude around the green, an attitude which can be summed up in two words: 'Sink it.' It's the same with putting, where the most common – and absolutely inexcusable – error among weekend golfers is to leave the ball short of the hole.

All of these problems can be addressed with an aggressive approach to the game. The aggressive golfer plays with a positive outlook that translates into a smooth, unhurried swing and a voracious hunger for the bottom of the cup. And that translates into lower scores.

I can see you saying to yourself, 'That's easy for Greg Norman to say.' And I can understand why you feel that way. You figure I'm this big, strong Australian guy who was born with tons of talent to swing fearlessly at every teeshot and gun at every flag.

Well, let me tell you, you don't have to be big, strong or even Australian to play aggressive golf. You don't even have to be highly talented – you simply have to know how to make optimum use of the ability you have. Aggressiveness comes not from genetics or environment, it comes from

Palmer, Nicklaus and Ballesteros – three very different personalities, three different swings, yet each of them knows how and when to play aggressively.

within. And when I say 'within', the last thing I mean is ego.

I've seen lots of guys play ego golf. In fact, occasionally, I still hit an ego shot or two myself. But those are bad shots, even when they're played perfectly. Ego shots are attempted by people who think they are better players than they actually are.

Let's face it, to a greater or lesser extent, we're all susceptible to ego – we're all victims of our best shots. If on one occasion in my career I was able to slam a 1-iron 260 yards over water to within a foot of the flag, I have a strong and pleasant mental record of that shot, and when I come to a similar situation, I'll naturally call on that memory. If my ego then takes over, I'll say to myself, 'I hit that beautiful high 1-iron back in 1986; I can do it again now.'

That's not aggressiveness, it's naivety. Ninety-nine times out of a hundred, such shots fall short of expectations. In my case, the 1-iron may miss the green, maybe even go in the water. In such a situation, a smooth, smart swing at one of my fairway woods is the wisely aggressive choice.

Everyone makes an ego mistake once in a while, but only a foolish player does it often. Such a golfer bases his shots not on wise course management but on self-delusion and wishful thinking. When he runs into trouble, he typically reacts badly. He can't accept his own incompetence, so he attempts a recovery shot that's equally beyond his reach. This frustrated, desperate demeanour only leads him into worse trouble.

Know Thyself

True aggressiveness is based not on self-idolatry or self-pity. It is based on self-knowledge.

When people ask me how I'm able to play with such boldness and assurance, I give them only one answer: I know exactly what my skills are, and I trust them.

I play golf the same way I drive a car. Some would say I go too fast and take corners too tight, but I know what the car can do and what I can do. I've done a lot of driving, I've talked to race car drivers, and even spent some time on race tracks learning advanced techniques of acceleration, braking and handling. What I've learned has given me confidence, and my driving experience has added more confidence. As a result, every time I get behind the wheel I stretch my skills to a point that is equal to that confidence. It's a high point, and it makes me an aggressive driver. But I'm only as aggressive as I am knowledgeable and experienced. If I were to spend a month at a racing driver's course, I'd learn more, have greater skill to trust, and then I'd drive even more aggressively than I do now.

It's the same way in golf. Wise aggressiveness is simply a reflection of your confidence in what you know you can do. And the nicest part is that in golf you can take this aggressive approach whether your handicap is scratch or 36.

The first step towards getting that feeling is to make an absolutely honest evaluation of your current skills. This can be a tough, perhaps even unpleasant exercise – sort of like hearing your voice on a tape-recorder for the first time – but it's vital. Before you can attack a golf course or improve your game, you must have a firm and realistic idea of the skills you now possess and the areas you need to strengthen.

You can begin your self-appraisal on the most basic level, by charting the distances you hit each of the clubs in your bag. Go to a practice area, hit several balls with each club, and step off the carrying distances, then take the average of those distances for each club. Do *not* measure only the best shots – use all of them, and then compute the average. This is part of being honest, and it's the only way you'll get an accurate idea of your ability. (See p.20 for fuller details.)

Next, take a hard look at the various aspects of your game and rate your abilities from tee to green. Don't compare yourself against the pros or against any standard of perfection. Just rate the elements of your game against each other within the context of *your* game. For example, let's say you're

Aggressive golf begins with an honest appraisal of your current ability with every club in the bag.

a 15-handicapper. That means you're a slightly better than average golfer. But it doesn't mean that every aspect of your game is exactly at that slightly-better-than-average level.

So take a pencil and paper, and make the following list: driver, fairway woods, long irons, middle irons, short irons, wedge play, bunker play, chipping, putting and trouble play. Then give a 'handicap' to each of those elements of your game. You may be a 6-handicap at driving but a 20 on the putting green, or vice versa. You may be a 2-handicap chipper but a 30-handicap sand player. (If you don't want to do the list on a handicap basis, just rate each of your abilities on a scale of one to ten, with ten the best.)

I still go through this exercise periodically. When this book went to press, I rated my driving, long approaches (woods and long irons) and sand play as the strengths of my game (in the 9 range). Slightly behind them I listed my chipping, putting and scrambling abilities (7 to 8). Next came my middle-iron approaches (7), and finally my wedge play (6). This analysis told me that my first priority was to work on my shots from 50 to 100 yards.

For the final part of your analysis, answer these questions about the character of your game.

1. Are you basically a flat swinger who tends to pick the ball off the turf with little or no divot, or are you more of an upright swinger, with a steep downward hit that takes big, deep divots?

2. In general do you hit the ball from right-to-left, left-to-right, dead straight or on a variety of paths?

3. What is the trajectory of your shots? Do you generally hit the ball high, low or about average?

4. When you miss a green with your approach shot, where does your ball usually finish – left of the green, right, long or short?

5. In the short game, are you best at playing hard, low, punchy shots or soft, high ones?

6. Of all the clubs in your bag, which is your favourite? Your second favourite? Which do you like least? Second least?

The answers to these questions, along with the ratings of your skills and the yardages you hit your clubs, will all fit on one piece of paper. And that piece of paper will be the beginning of the most powerful weapon you can have: an aggressive game plan.

The Fruit of Self-Analysis: Confidence

Having honestly analysed your game, you will know exactly what you can and can't do. However meagre your skills may be, you will *know* that you have them and that you have certain strengths and abilities. The affirmation of that knowledge will give you something that most amateur golfers never develop – confidence.

And it's the best kind of confidence. It's not that egotistical overconfidence that prompts foolishly bold play; nor is it the underconfidence that most amateurs display. It's 'a quiet arrogance', according to Peter Alliss, a quality which he claims is evident in the eyes of all great champions.

This knowledge also gives you a feeling of inner serenity, a sense of realism that insulates you from the ups and downs that the game throws your way.

In 1973 I was eighteen years old and I hadn't developed this serenity, but a good friend of mine, Roger Dwyer, had. Roger, a fine player with whom I worked at Precision Golf Forgings in Australia, was older than I and understood me better than anyone at that time. When I qualified for my first Australian Open, he agreed to caddie for me.

Although I was an amateur, after three rounds I had an outside chance to win. On the 10th hole of the final day my second shot found the front bunker, and while Roger moved to the back of the green and parked the buggy at the bottom of the slope I settled into the sand.

The next thing I knew, I had hit my bunker shot a bit thin and the ball had rolled across the green and down the slope where it bumped into my buggy, which Roger had left unattended. In those days, that was an automatic two-stroke penalty.

I was seething with anger as I chipped the ball back up the slope and finally holed out for an eight that wiped me from contention. As we left the next tee I turned furiously to Roger and demanded to know why he had been careless enough to leave my buggy where he had.

'Do you know what you have cost me?' I said angrily.

Poor but wise Roger. He put an arm over my shoulder and said, 'One day you are going to be a great player. Rome was not built in a day and you will have many more bad breaks. I'm sorry.'

For the first and only time on a golf course I burst into tears. I grabbed my towel from my golf bag and draped it over my head to hide my misery. On the next hole I took a double-bogey.

Calmness wasn't a feature of my game those days, when I had plenty of talent but not much sense. But in the years since, I've often reflected back on the wisdom of Roger's words. Knowledge and understanding of my game has brought an inner confidence and perspective. Today, if I am half the player Roger said I would be, it's because I have gained a little more talent, and a lot more serenity.

Goodness knows, this inner calm has helped me throughout my career. Sometimes I think I have an almost perverse love of being down, even being defeated, because I know it will spur me on to greater things.

I vividly recall my first major setback, at the 1979 Australian Open. I was twenty-four and I had an excellent chance to win my first national title. The tournament was played at the Metropolitan Golf Club, and as I came to the 72nd hole, I needed a par to force a playoff with Jack Newton.

After a long, straight drive I hit my second shot into good position on the green thirty feet below the hole. From there I rolled my first putt four feet past the hole and then, unfortunately, missed the putt to tie.

The next day the Australian papers all carried the same story: 'Norman lacks the guts to become a champion. He missed his chance, and now he'll never win a big one.' When I saw those headlines, I was livid. I vowed to give those newspapers a lesson, and the next year I did. Not only did I win the Australian Open, I won the French Open, the Scandinavian Open and the World Match Play Championship as well.

What adversity helps you do – forces you to do – is focus on a goal. And if you have an accurate appraisal of – and thus a confidence in – your game, and a goal in your sights, you can reach that goal and beyond.

Goals Are the Fuel for Progress

I've built my career on a succession of goals. Hitting them – and sometimes missing them narrowly – has been the fuel, the impetus that has taken me from one level up to the next. When at age fifteen I tagged along with my Mom to the Virginia Golf Club, a couple of miles from our home in Queensland, I knew nothing about golf. But after caddieing for Mom a couple of times, I decided I should give it a try. After all, Mom was pretty good at the game, and I figured if she could do it, so could I.

One day I borrowed her clubs and went on to the course. Well, the results were mixed. A few went straight, a lot went badly off line. But every now and then I caught one on the screws. What a feeling that was!

So I guess my first goal was to experience more of those long straight ones. I went at it with everything, hitting hundreds of shots with Mom's clubs after she finished her rounds. When I got my first set of clubs and my first official handicap – 27 – my goal was clear: get that handicap down to zero. One year – and a few thousand practice balls – later I was down to 11, and a year after that, I got to scratch.

My next goal was to win a tournament, and at age eighteen I did it in the 1973 Queensland junior championship, where rounds of 73–74 gave me a five-stroke margin. Few victories have ever satisfied me more. It gave me the hope to achieve another goal – to turn pro.

For a couple of years I worked as an apprentice professional, and in 1975 won the Queensland trainee championship in a playoff. The following year, I won it, I think, by fifteen strokes. That whetted my appetite for bigger things, a true professional victory.

I got it a year later in the 1976 West Lakes Classic over a field that included Bruce Crampton and David Graham. This led me to want more victories – in places other than Australia. Gradually I got them – in Japan, Scotland, Hong Kong, England, France, Sweden and Wales. Along the way, I also won the big one at home, the aforementioned 1980 Australian Open. By 1982 I had a new goal – I wanted to show I could win on the big circuit – the US PGA Tour.

I joined that circuit in early 1983, and in my first start I nearly hit my goal. Coming from six strokes back on the final day, I tied Mike Nicolette after seventy-two holes of Arnold Palmer's Bay Hill Classic. But Mike won the playoff. That disappointment just doubled my resolve.

It was another year before I got my victory but it was a good one – a five-stroke win in the Kemper Open, followed shortly thereafter by the Canadian Open championship. And these successes whetted my appetite for the biggest victory of all – a major championship.

I almost got it that same 1984 season in the US Open at Winged Foot. A lengthy par-saving putt on the final hole enabled me to tie Fuzzy Zoeller. But the next day, I lost the eighteen-hole playoff.

Two years later, I came painfully close again, in the 1986 Masters, where Jack Nicklaus's fantastic 30 on the final nine edged me and Tom Kite by a stroke.

I also led the 1986 US Open going into the final round, but that Sunday just wasn't my day, and I finished in a tie for 12th. With two disappointments in the year's first two championships, I boarded the Concorde for Turnberry, Scotland, more determined than ever. While in the air I told my wife, Laura, that I was going to lead the British Open all four rounds and win it going away.

And I did. Coming down that 18th fairway at Turnberry, I was choking back the tears. Somehow, although I knew it was happening and I had earned it, I couldn't believe all the years of hard work had finally come to fruition.

Victory in my first major immediately put me in a mind to do only one thing – win my second major – and at Inverness Country Club a month later, I thought I had it. But this game of golf we all love so much does not always love us back. Over the last nine holes of the 1986 PGA Championship I saw a four-stroke lead slip out of my hands, then watched the title vanish as Bob Tway holed his miraculous bunker shot on the 72nd hole.

Needless to say, I was enormously disappointed. But not a half-hour after I walked off that final green, the sting was gone and the events of the day were behind me. I was satisfied that I had played a lot of good shots on that Sunday, and I knew that as long as I had not lost confidence in my game, then no other player, shot or event could lose it for me.

In the press interview I said my only concern was the next tournament. I in fact predicted I'd win that one and the one after that too. Well, I didn't win that week or the week after. But I did win the week after that, and the week after that, and the week after that. In fact, less than a month after my loss in the PGA I began a string of six straight victories throughout Great Britain, Europe and Australia, the longest such streak since Byron Nelson's eleven consecutive wins in 1945.

During that stretch, each victory pumped me up for another one. My goal at that point was simple – keep the string going. But when Mike Harwood shot a course-record 64 in the final round of the Australian PGA, he pipped me by two strokes and ended my streak. That experience left me more than a little bit flat for my last event of the year, the Western Australian Open.

I was tired. I had played nine weeks in a row, something I'll never do again, and I had won tournaments during most of those weeks. But, more importantly, I had no more goals, no more mountains to climb in 1986. Or so I thought.

After two rounds I was several strokes off the pace. That evening I placed a call to Laura in Brisbane, and told her I was having trouble getting fired up to play. 'Find me some motivation,' I said. Her answer came immediately. She said she had seen an article in the paper that said, if I could win in this final event, I'd lead the Australian Tour money-winning list. 'Wouldn't it be nice', she said, 'to lead two money lists on two Tours in the same year?' (I had already won the money title on the US Tour.) 'That's something no one has ever done.'

That was all the motivation I needed. I shot 66 in the third round, then 68 in the final to beat Terry Gale by a stroke. It was the last of my ten victories in 1986.

The biggest year of my career was followed immediately by my biggest disappointment, in the 1987 Masters. I didn't think that it was possible for any player to suffer a second knockout punch such as the one Tway gave me at Inverness. And certainly I didn't think it could happen twice in a row, in consecutive major championships. But it did. In the 1987 Masters when Larry Mize holed out a 140-foot pitch shot for birdie on the second hole of sudden death, I was absolutely stunned. I had been facing a 30-foot birdie putt, and with Mize having missed the green with his approach, I figured the worst I could possibly get out of the hole was a tie. But in the ball went, and when my own attempt slid by, I had lost my second major in a row in excruciating fashion.

That was without question the most demoralising day of my career. And I don't mind telling you, it took a bit more time getting over that shot than it did Tway's blast. Mize's shot was nearly twice as difficult as Tway's.

But the way I look at it, I probably needed an extra boot in the rear to get me going in 1987. As far as I'm concerned, I'm due for at least two majors to come my way. Over the long haul, the breaks have a way of evening out, assuming you're tough enough to hang in and keep playing hard. That's exactly what I plan to do. And although it's too early to tell, I'm confident that my disappointment at Augusta will ultimately have the same positive effect that my other near-misses have had: eventually, I'll be back, and stronger than ever.

You'll forgive the personal digression, I hope, because it's intended to make a point. If you have a goal and pursue it aggressively, you'll achieve it, no matter what kinds of breaks this crazy game throws your way.

Setting Aggressive Goals

Setting goals for your game is an art. The trick is in setting them at the right level – neither too low nor too high. A good goal should be lofty enough to inspire hard work yet near enough to provide realistic hope of attainment. If, for instance, you're a 15-handicapper at the start of the season, there's not much point in aspiring to a season-end handicap of 14. For most people that single stroke is not sufficient motivation. It's like going on a diet to lose one pound.

On the other hand, you probably don't want to set a goal to become a 5-handicap either. Unless you're possessed of unusual time and talent, ten strokes is far too tall an order for one year. A good compromise would be to shoot for a handicap of 9 – the allure of a single digit next to your name, yet within comfortable reach of your present level.

Your analysis of your game – that sheet of paper with all the numbers and answers – is a blueprint for your goal setting, but you must first answer one more question: how hard do you want to work?

Basically, every golfer, assuming he is physically able, has two choices: he can make the best of his current method or he can try to overhaul that method. Of the two, the first is far less taxing but offers a smaller reward. The second demands much more but yields much more.

Our friend the 15-handicapper could choose the first path and might be able to lower his handicap to 9 without making any major changes in his swing and without undue time and trouble. But he wouldn't get much better than a 9. Alternatively, assuming he were to choose the overhaul route, he might expect to get down to a 5-handicap, perhaps even lower, but only after a lot of hard work.

The first option generally requires great attention to the scoring aspects of golf – the short game, sand play, putting and trouble shots, plus practice or play at least once a week. The second option entails thorough study of all aspects of the game, possibly reinforced with lessons from a competent PGA professional, and it certainly involves thousands of practice balls, plus on-course practice or play two or more times per week.

So ask yourself how much desire you have. Then set your general strategy – basically choose one of the two routes – and begin to set some specific *interim* goals as part of that strategy.

Set easy ones first. Let's say you chose the first route, to make the best of your current method, and let's say you're that 15-handicapper in search of a 9. Clearly, you'll have to begin working on your short game and putting, but before you do, set yourself an interim handicap target of 12. If, on your home course, you usually shoot about 87, then reorient yourself to an average score of 84. And if par for your course is 72 or 70 or whatever, forget it. Stop thinking about the course's par and instead focus on your own personal par – 84.

You can do this by going through the course, hole by hole, and deciding on which holes you should make pars and where you should expect bogeys. This is far more reasonable, and motivational, than playing against eighteen pars. A personal par of 84 gives you a reachable goal, something you can pursue with confidence and aggressiveness.

In determining your par and bogey holes, go back to your analysis. If your favourite club is the 7-iron, and if one of the par-3 holes calls for a 7-iron teeshot, surely you'll want to plan for a par on that hole. If you habitually play a draw, you'll probably want to plan for pars on the right-to-left holes and bogeys on the left-to-rights. If you hit a high ball, you might feel comfortable planning for bogey on the into-the-wind holes.

You probably will never shoot your goal score for each of the eighteen holes in a single round, but these eighteen mini-goals will give you plenty of room for aspiration. Your double-bogey sixes won't get you disgusted, and many of your par fours will feel like birdies. It probably won't take you long to start shooting that new par-84. Once you have a couple of 84s or better under your belt, set the second goal of 81. Readjust your scores for the individual holes so that you have eighteen comfortably attainable targets totalling 81, and then go at them again. Don't be surprised if it's even easier the second time – you may even see a few scores in the 70s.

Now let's say your goal is not tied to your handicap. Let's say you simply want to become a more consistent player. Once again, take a look at your self-analysis. This time, see which areas of your game are the weakest. If chipping is your Achilles' heel, adopt the method explained in Chapter 8 of this book, and practise it with a bold 'think "sink"' attitude. This is exactly what I did. At the end of 1984 chipping was clearly the worst part of my game. So I marched myself to a practice green and spent hours and hours refining the rough spots.

If that sounds arduous and dull, put some fun into it by charting your progress. Take twenty balls and begin by practising routine twenty-foot chip shots. See how many of the twenty you can knock into the hole. Chances are, you won't make any at first, but you should set yourself a goal of sinking at least one. Once you can sink one out of twenty consistently, try to sink an average of two out of twenty, then three, then four. When you can sink four out of twenty from twenty feet, you'll find that chipping is no longer the weakest part of your game!

Or let's take another goal – you want to win your club championship. Again, go through your game analysis, and match it to your course. Determine the spots where you want to play aggressively and where you want to play safe. Don't be afraid to avoid situations where you'd have to play your less-than-favourite shots.

If, for example, you're one of those players with a flattish swing and a picking action through the ball, you probably have a particular aversion to the rough, so think about the areas of your course where the highest grass grows, and then plot a strategy which avoids it at all cost. If that means going off the tee with a 3-iron instead of a driver, it may be your wisest move. If you're a downward hitter, you may have some extra difficulty with fairway bunkers, so make note of the worst ones on your course and in your matches be sure to give them a wide berth.

This type of strategy is akin to the tennis tactic of running around one's backhand, avoiding the shot that is not your strength. It may not seem particularly aggressive, but it actually is. You have to think of golf as a big chess game where each move sets up the next move. Even better, think of it as outdoor snooker, where the intent of each stroke is to leave the ball in ideal position for the stroke that will follow. Sometimes, you may have to play what seems like a cautious shot, in order to set up an attack.

For instance, if you're very accurate with a full pitching wedge but not very good with partial wedge shots, then on holes where you have to lay up short of the green, there's no point in trying to slug your ball up close where you'll have to hit that partial shot. Instead, you should be sure to leave yourself enough room so that you can play that full wedge into the green.

The pros do this all the time, and Johnny Miller is one of the best at it. He knows that he's as precise as anyone in the world at hitting a golf ball 110 yards – exactly 110 yards. He figures that from that distance he can put his shot within six feet of the pin more often than not. So on par-fives where Johnny knows he can't get home in two he simply asks his caddie, 'What's the yardage to the 110 point?' Then he hits whatever club he needs to get to that distance – he may hit as little as a 6- or 7-iron, secure in the knowledge that the next shot will give him a short birdie putt. *That's* aggressive golf – using your strongest tools as often and as effectively as possible.

Reinforce on the Course

No matter what your goal – to lower your handicap, strengthen a particular part of your game, win more weekend nassaus, or whatever – you should give yourself some room with easily achievable stepping-stone goals, and devise a plan of consistent practice and play that takes you towards those goals.

'Consistent' is the key word. If you want to hit your goals, you have to stick to your plan. It's no different from adhering to a business plan with the goal of making a certain profit, or to a diet with a goal of a slimmer figure. Even if the plan is a good one, an aggressive one, you have to work at it.

Fortunately, in golf at least, there are a few tricks you can use to keep moving forward. Positive reinforcement is what the psychologists like to call them.

For me, this reinforcement occurs right on the golf course, while I'm playing. I talk to myself. Sometimes silently, sometimes loud enough for me and my caddie, Pete Bender, to hear, and sometimes loud enough for the whole gallery to listen in. But I talk to myself all the time.

The tougher the challenge, the more I talk. When I have a long approach shot to a tough pin position, for instance, as I step up to the ball I'll say something like 'You know the shot you want to hit. You've hit it a thousand times before. So go ahead and do it.'

That's a necessary peptalk from the guy who knows me best, and believe me, it works. When you're standing on the edge of a tough shot, it's good to hear words of encouragement, even if they're only coming from inside.

I also talk to myself *after* shots. When, in the final round of the 1986 British Open, I hit a 4-iron that struck the flagstick, and finished a couple of feet away, I said, loud enough for Pete to hear, 'Damn, Greg, I'm pretty impressed by that one.' Reinforcement once again.

You can use verbalisation whether you're on the practice range, on the first tee of a big match or anywhere on the course. It's one of the best ways to psych yourself up for the shot ahead, and then congratulate yourself – out loud if you want – on your success in pulling it off. (Just try to do it in a gracious way that won't upset your playing companions.)

Verbalising something is similar to writing it down – it helps you to remember. You don't want to dwell on your shots – good ones or bad ones. But you do want to file the good ones away for future reference. That way you'll be able to bring them back as part of another reinforcement technique – visualisation.

If you want to play aggressive golf, you also have to be ready to struggle constantly against a special challenge. For each shotmaking situation, you must consider both the dull, safe, pedestrian route or routes, and the more audacious paths as well. For each of those alternative shots, you should be able to dig back into your memory and call forth a fine shot – complete with trajectory, flight path, bounce and roll. You should then be able to look at it in cold comparison to the demands facing you, and decide whether you want to try it again. Having reviewed these mini-movies, you must select the best one to replay. And do so in the few seconds you have to play your shot.

This is all done through visualisation. You envision the ideal shot, 'seeing' the takeoff, flight and landing of the ball in vivid detail. Then you recall successful similar shots from your past, and draw confidence from those earlier successes. I can think of favourite shots for virtually every situation I face, and I call them forth each time I play. I'm not sure where in my brain I store those memories, but if I start to lose my mind, I hope that part goes last!

Managing Your Aggressiveness

The challenge for an aggressive golfer, however, is to check his enthusiasm. As I said, we're all victims of our best shots. When forced to ask ourselves, 'Can I do it or can't I?', the answer is invariably 'Yes I can.' So when you visualise your ideal shot, be sure that 'ideal' is *your* ideal, not the ultimate shot. Be sure it's a shot that you have played successfully several times. And when you do play a difficult or daring shot, be sure that the potential reward is in line with the gamble you take.

The best strategist I've ever seen is Jack Nicklaus. His wisdom on the golf course is without equal. Although his overall game management is a shade on the conservative side, he's certainly not afraid to play a bold shot when he perceives that the reward is worth the risk. I'm still in awe of one shot he played against me in the semi-final of the 1986 World Matchplay in Wentworth, England.

We were all even at the 13th hole of the morning round. Number 13 at Wentworth is a lengthy par-five, and after a good teeshot, Jack was staring at a 290-yard approach, with out of bounds on both sides. Now, Jack is the greatest 3-wood player ever to lose, but I could barely believe my eyes when I saw him take out a 3-wood. And my incredulity increased as I watched him pummel that ball, at age forty-six and a half, all the way on to the green. I didn't think Jack could still do those things. But he *knew* he could, and he knew just when to show me. I eventually won that match, but not until we'd had a good battle down to the 36th hole. Playing with Nicklaus is like taking a graduate seminar in golf-course management.

Fortunately, for everyone who will never get the opportunity to play with Jack, there are a couple of other ways to develop course smarts. The first is to do what football coaches do with their teams – rerun the game tapes.

I'm an analyst at heart, and after every tournament, I conduct a little post-mortem. It's a private session that I seldom share with anyone. I go over my performance with a mental microscope, examining my mistakes. With each poor shot I ask myself this question: 'Was it a mistake of judgement or of execution?' The answers give me a picture of how I'm doing both mentally and physically. If I discover that I've made a repeated physical error – such as pulling a lot of putts or losing teeshots to the left – then I'll head for the practice tee and immediately focus on that problem. If, on the other hand, I find that I've made a lot of mental errors – let's say I've been overly aggressive – I make a conscious effort to think twice before taking my next leap. If my analysis tells me I've played too cautiously, I'll start firing at a few more flags. I go through these sessions even when I win, asking myself what I did right as well as wrong.

This type of analysis puts you in a positive, forward-thinking frame of mind for the next day, the next week. Just ask Ray Floyd. He went through a sort of automotive analysis with his wife Maria, the Sunday evening after he blew to a 77 and lost the 1986 Westchester Classic. For three hours they rode in a car together and discussed that round, picking out the mistakes and discussing the cures. By the time they got where they were going – Southampton, Long Island – Raymond had a whole new attitude. And he immediately used that attitude to take him to victory, at age forty-three, in the US Open at Shinnecock Hills.

The other way to control your course management is to analyse yourself on the day of your round. I get a slightly different feeling each time I step to the practice tee, and by the end of the twenty minutes or so I spend there, I have a definite impression of how sharp or flat I'll be that day. If I'm flat, I'll need something big to happen to put me in an aggressive mode – a couple of early birdies, a long putt or perhaps a holed sand shot. Otherwise, I won't try anything fancy or particularly aggressive. If on the other hand I feel strong and sharp, I may play a 70–30 brand of golf (aggressive 70 per cent of the time, cautious 30 per cent). It's on such days that I've shot record low scores – a 62 at Las Vegas, a 62 at Kemper, a 63 at Turnberry.

So try to get a feel for your state of mind and body during practice and the early part of your round. Then go with your day – if you feel so-so, play it safe; if you feel great, be aggressive. Just try not to let yourself get out of hand. On a couple of those low rounds I shot, I suspect I could have been a stroke or two lower still if I had been a hair more cautious towards the end of the round.

A good example is the final round of the 1986 Masters. Jack Nicklaus had blown past everyone and I was three or four strokes behind him. Then I birdied the 14th. Then 15. Then 16, and suddenly I was within a stroke of Jack with two holes to go.

On 17 I let my teeshot get away from me, and it settled under a couple of tall pines. That left me with a 160-yard shot that had to be punched low enough to get under some branches and yet somehow land and stick on the slippery green. This was one of those situations when laying-up was an option. I could have bumped the ball up short of the green, but that would have left a tough little flip on to the green in the hope of a one-putt par. Instead I decided to play the low-percentage super-aggressive shot. A main reason was the fact that I was 'on', hot off three straight birdies. So I took a 9-iron, punched it crisply, and it came off just as planned. The ball finished fifteen feet from the hole.

When something like that happens, I talk to myself again and say, 'All right, Greg, now you owe it to yourself to sink this putt – that was too good a shot to waste.' Sure enough the putt went in and I made my fourth bird in a row. As I walked off that green, one thought was in my mind. Make one more birdie, and you're the Masters Champion.

On the tee at 18, I reached for my driver, anxious to hit the longest, hardest teeshot of my life. Boy was I pumped up. But Pete, my caddie, knew the symptoms all too well, and he quickly throttled me back. 'Take the 3-wood and put it in good position,' he said, 'then we'll attack.'

Of course he was right, and I was able to hit a strong yet safe drive up the middle. From there I had roughly 190 uphill yards to the final green. A birdie to win, a par to get into a playoff with Jack.

After four straight birdies, par was the farthest thing from my mind. And in retrospect, that was a foolish way to be thinking. My options on that shot were two – take a 5-iron and hit a strong, commercial shot to the centre of the green, leaving the ball twenty feet or so below the pin which was positioned at the back; or take a 4-iron and try to feather the ball in a soft, high, slight fade, so that it would land near the pin and stop dead, leaving a short birdie putt.

At that point I was convinced it was in the cards for me to win. I was playing too well and nothing could stop me. The fact was, I had allowed myself to get too pumped up. (Incidentally, it's my feeling that Seve Ballesteros lost that same tournament for the same reason. People always will point to the 4-iron he pulled into the pond at 15, but what undid him, I think, was his overcelebratory reaction to the brilliant shot he hit to the 13th green. I think Seve felt he had sewn up the tournament with that shot – and he hadn't.) But back to me. I chose the 4-iron and went for the whole show. Thirty seconds later my ball was in the right-hand gallery. Ten minutes later I had a share of second place with Tom Kite.

My point is that you should go with the way you feel, but temper your temper. Don't allow yourself to get so pumped up that you burst. If the shot is not comfortably within your power, you shouldn't play it, unless the situation is do or die. If I had needed birdie to tie Jack, my shot would have been the right one. But needing only a par, I was too aggressive.

Monitor your aggressiveness, with pre-round analysis of your demeanour and post-round analysis of your performance, and you'll have a good grip on bold course management. You'll be playing the ideal 50–50 brand of aggressive golf.

Layer Success with More Success

In this crazy game, things don't always work out according to a Hollywood script, so it's important to try to maintain some perspective. The fact is, on that Masters Sunday, they came about as close to the ideal script as possible. Jack Nicklaus was a glorious champion, winning his sixth time at age forty-six. It just wasn't *my* ideal script. In pro golf – and when battling this game in general – you tend to lose more often than you win.

So when you hit a disappointment, step aside for a moment, close your eyes, take a deep breath, and then do your damnedest to forget what happened. Focus on the next shot or the next round, not on what just happened. If that doesn't work, repeat to yourself the old line of Lloyd Mangrum: 'Remember,' he said, 'it's not your life, it's not your wife; it's only a game.' This is one of the greatest favours you can do yourself. It's part of being a wisely aggressive player. Remember, if you're one of ten players disappointed on Sunday and you're the first to snap out of it, you have an important edge on the other nine come next week.

Besides, in failing a test and falling short of your goal, you can often benefit as surely as if you were to reach that goal. You benefit by learning. In 1984 one of my goals was to win that US Open. When I got to the 72nd fairway, however, I found myself in a situation I had never encountered. For the first time in my life I was *scared* of a shot. It was as if that final green was a dark room and I was a little boy, afraid to open the door. Yes, I'll admit I choked on the 6-iron I hit in there. But I salvaged par on that hole, and I have never choked on a shot since then.

Leading all four majors in one year in 1986 was something no one had ever done, and it was a satisfying achievement for me. Failing to win three out of the four was not satisfying. Nor, to be sure, was the experience at the 1987 Masters. But through those disappointments I learned a lot. I learned that I am a good enough player to lead all four majors in a single year, and to hold or share the final-round lead in five majors in a row. And if I can lead them during those final rounds, certainly I can lead them after the tournaments are over. All four of them. In the same year. Yes, I learned that I am capable of winning the Grand Slam.

That is my goal, and will be my goal as long as I feel it is within the reach of my game. I may never achieve it, but the way I see it, as long as I am the only man in golf who honestly believes the Grand Slam is within his reach, I am the guy with the best chance of achieving it. That's the aggressor's edge.

CHAPTER 2

A Solid Base

PRE-SWING FUNDAMENTALS

The evening of 19 July 1986 marks one of the truly special experiences of my life. The scene was the main dining room of the Turnberry Hotel, set high on a hill overlooking Scotland's Firth of Clyde. No, this was not the night of my victory in the Open Championship at Turnberry. It was the night before.

As Laura and I finished our dinner, we watched the late-setting sun cast its long shadows across the rugged land below. On that wind-thrashed links known as Ailsa, 150 of the world's best golfers had spent the previous three days in competition.

With the final round left to play, I had a one-stroke lead over Tommy Nakajima. It was the third time that year I had held the 54-hole lead in a major championship. Earlier in the season, however, at the Masters and then at the US Open, I had seen those leads disappear.

'Doubt' is not in my vocabulary, but I must admit I did wonder when my day would come.

Laura and I were sipping our coffee in pensive silence when I felt a tap on my shoulder. I turned around and was surprised to see the smiling face of the man who had beaten me in such dramatic fashion at Augusta, Jack Nicklaus.

'Do you mind if I join you for a second?' he said.

'Please do,' said I, swivelling my chair to the side as Jack pulled one over for himself. Then he gave me the greatest pep talk of my life.

'No one wants you to win this championship more than I do,' he said. 'You're a fine player, and you're playing well this week. Heck, you've been playing well all year and you deserve to win. But if you don't mind, I'd like to give you one bit of advice for tomorrow.'

'I'd love to hear it,' I said, feeling equal parts flattered and stunned. This, after all, was like a dream, a fantasy. Here was my lifelong idol, the undisputed finest golfer in history, coming to me on the eve of the tournament I most wanted to win, and asking if I'd allow him to offer me the key to victory!

In the next split-second I wondered what he would say. Something about patience or concentration or dealing with final-round pressure? Surely, no one knows more about the nuances of competitive psychology than Jack. But his advice had nothing to do with such subtleties.

'The only thing you need to work on tomorrow', he said, 'is your grip. Check your grip pressure before every shot, and be sure you don't get too tight.' After some minor elaboration, he wished me luck and left.

My grip! Imagine that. Jack Nicklaus shares his precious advice on how to win a major championship, and what does he tell me? Check my grip.

And of course he was right. The next day, I used

that advice and won the British Open by five strokes. But it was the nature of his advice, in a larger sense, that has been of even greater and more enduring value to me. In the weeks and months following that victory I often recalled my chat with Jack, and I realised how it reinforced my own philosophy of golf, a philosophy that will be one of the keynotes of this book: *you must adhere to the basics*.

I'm often asked how I was able to take up the game of golf at age fifteen and become a scratch handicap within two years, and I always give the same answer: I developed good basics, and I stuck with them. It sounds overly simple – and that's exactly the way it *should* sound.

You must simplify this game. Learning to play good golf is like trying to put together a huge picture puzzle. The more pieces you can fit together properly in the early stages, the faster and easier the rest of the puzzle will come together.

I have a set of fundamentals that I check and recheck every time I lace up my shoes, and I want to share them with you just as Jack Nicklaus shared that one bit of basic advice with me. The remainder of this chapter will include all of my pre-swing basics, and in each chapter after this one, I will begin with a section devoted *purely* to the basics. Read those sections alone, and you'll have all you need to know to become a very good golfer.

Each of Chapters 3 through 10 also includes sections entitled 'The Aggressor's Edge' and 'I Dare You', for everyone who wants to play the game as aggressively as I do. But these sections always follow the sections on the basics. That's the way it has to be. For trying to play aggressive golf without a firm foundation is like trying to launch a rocket from a lily pad.

So let's start building that foundation. And let's begin with the same fundamental that Jack Nicklaus impressed upon me – the grip.

The proper grip begins with your palms parallel and perpendicular to your target.

The Grip

Logic, simplicity and comfort – those are the three qualities I look for in every aspect of my game. If something makes sense, is uncomplicated and feels good, it probably works.

The only logical place to begin a discussion of the basics is with the grip. After all, that's the point where you connect yourself to the golf club, and every move you make in the swing will be a result, either directly or indirectly, of the way your hands meet the handle.

The simplest way to understand the proper grip is to clap your hands. Stand up, bend slightly from the waist, and let your hands hang naturally at your sides. Now, bring your hands flat together as if you were clapping.

Note a couple of things about this position. First, your palms are parallel – they're facing each other. Secondly, they're perpendicular to the ground. The back of your left hand (assuming you're a right-handed golfer) and the palm of your right are facing a point roughly 90 degrees to your left.

This is called a square position, and it is the beginning of a square grip, the ideal way to hold a golf club. If, in assuming your grip on the club, you can keep your palms parallel with your right palm facing the target, you'll give yourself a tremendous head start on the rest of your golf game.

A square grip leads naturally to a square address position which in turn produces an uncomplicated, efficient golf swing, a swing that has the best chance of returning the clubface squarely, powerfully and consistently to the back of the ball.

Unfortunately, most golfers begin with a grip that violates one or both of the rules of squareness. Either the palms aren't parallel, they aren't square or they aren't either of those things.

Check your own grip. Take your usual hold on the club and then simply open your hands so that your fingers point straight and you hold the clubshaft between your flattened palms. Are your palms facing? If they are not, then you're doing your game a disservice. If your palms aren't parallel, it means your hands are fighting each other during the swing. Your left hand might be trying to turn the club open on the backswing while your right hand resists, or your right hand might be trying to make a strong release into the ball while your left hand impedes it. When your hands aren't unified, you rob your swing of both accuracy and power.

Assuming your hands *are* parallel, take another look. Is your right palm facing the target, or is it pointing a bit down towards the ground or, more likely, up towards the sky? If it's pointing downwards, you have what's called a weak grip, and if it's pointed skyward your grip is strong. Neither is the ideal way to hold the club.

Of course it's one thing to hold the club with your hands open and your flat palms pressing together, and quite another to keep this square position while joining your hands and fastening your fingers securely around the club. That brings us to the question of the style of grip.

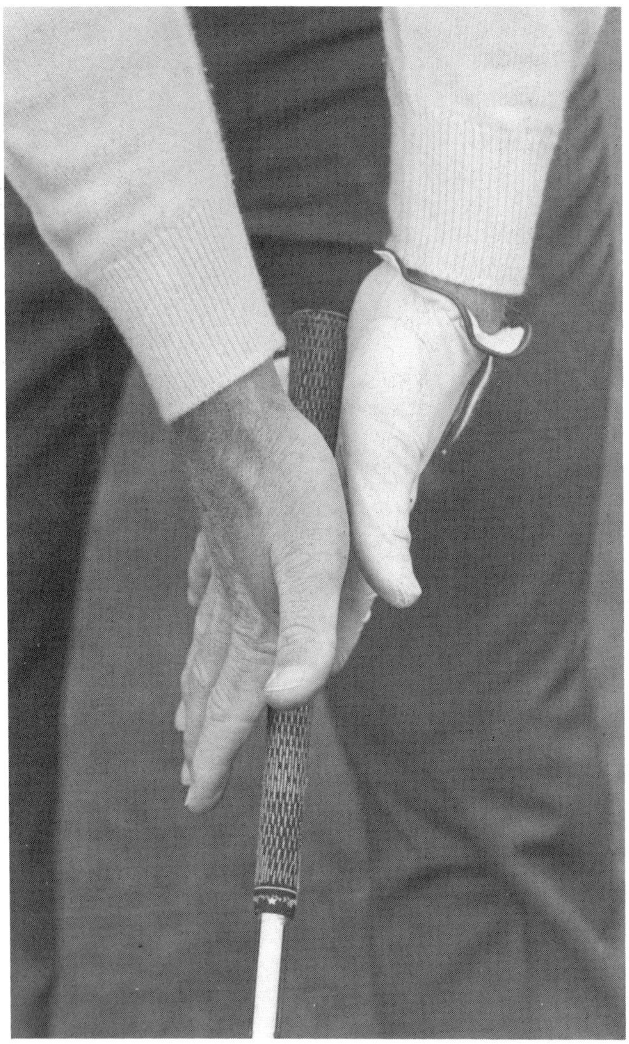

If they're tilted to your left, your grip is weak.

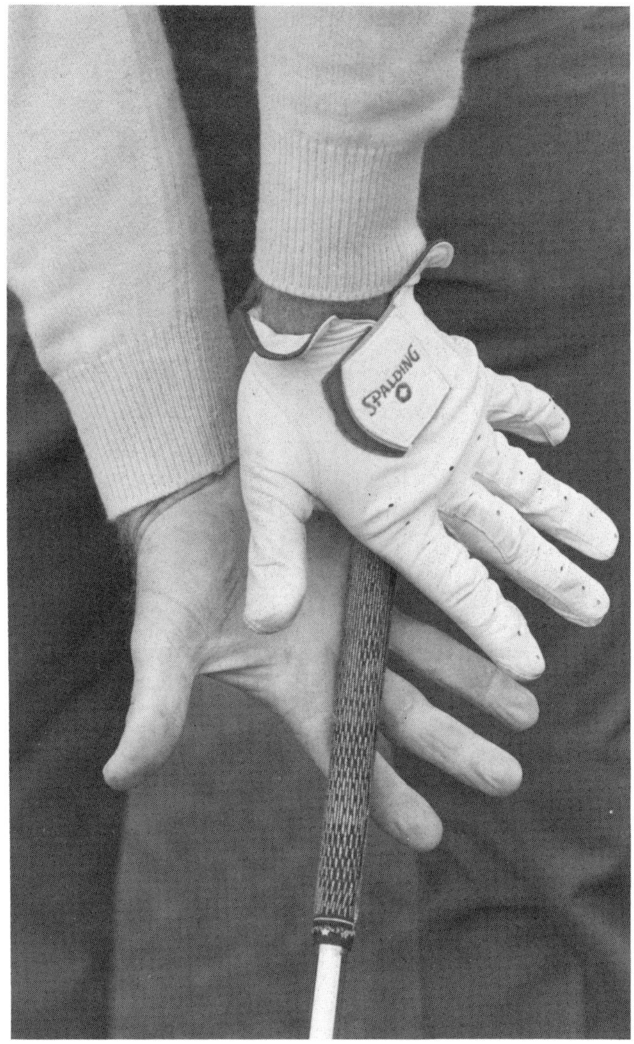

Too far to the right, and you have a strong grip.

Basically, you can assume the proper palms-parallel-and-square grip with a number of methods, including the ten-finger, the Vardon and the interlock. As far as I'm concerned, your choice depends purely on personal comfort.

For that reason – comfort – many people begin playing golf with a ten-finger grip. After all, that's the way they gripped baseball bats or cricket bats and just about anything else they've ever swung with two hands. Beyond this natural feeling, the ten-finger grip has one obvious advantage over other styles – all ten fingers are in touch with the club. This clearly enhances feel. But the grip has one major disadvantage as well – the hands are not joined together in any way. There is no unity. When the hands aren't linked, they're more apt to fight each other in the way I mentioned earlier.

The most widely accepted method of linking the hands is the overlapping or Vardon grip, named after six-times British Open Champion, Harry Vardon, who popularised it at the turn of the century. In this grip the little finger of the right hand overlaps the index finger of the left and rests on top of the groove formed between the index and middle fingers of the left hand. About two-thirds of all golfers, and an even higher percentage of professionals, use the Vardon grip.

However, I'm afraid I'm not one of them. Remember, comfort is the key, and for me the Vardon was not right. The reason is, for a tall and large-boned man, I have relatively small hands and feet. I wear size 9½ shoes, my glove size is medium, and I actually have short, stubby little fingers. Thus I was never comfortable trying to extend my little finger up and over my left hand. I just couldn't wed my hands securely with that grip.

When I began learning the game with Jack Nicklaus's book, *Golf My Way*, I was pleased to open up to the pages where Jack's hands were silhouetted in actual size. What a wonderful revelation to find that the Golden Bear's paws were no larger than mine! Immediately, I adopted Jack's grip – the interlock.

Interlock means that, instead of overlapping, that right-hand little finger interlaces with the left hand, threading between the index and middle fingers. It provides a secure and unified hold on the club, yet it's not as much of a stretch for the little finger as is the Vardon. For this reason, it's a good alternative for people with small hands.

But alas, after a few rounds of golf with the interlocking grip, I concluded that it wasn't right for me either. For some reason, it just didn't feel comfortable.

So I invented my own grip, which I'm revealing here in print for the first time. I call it the 'intermesh'. As far as I know, I'm the only professional golfer using it, and I haven't seen any amateurs with it either (except the handful of people I've converted).

Basically, instead of overlapping or interlocking that right-hand little finger, I poke it straight down into the bottom of the vee between my index and middle fingers. At the same time, the index finger of my left hand rests on the vee between the ring and little fingers of my right. This meshing method gives me a couple of big advantages. For one, my fingers actually fit together, just like gears meshing, and this binds the hands more securely than with any other method I've tried. For another, I'm able to get about nine and a half fingers on the club, more than with either the Vardon or interlocking grips.

My intermesh isn't for everyone, but if you're as short-fingered as I am, I encourage you to give it a try. It's unorthodox, but to me it's logical, it's simple and it's comfortable. My point is this: you can join your hands together any way you want – or not at all – as long as your palms are parallel and facing your target.

The way you actually lay the club across your palms is also to some extent a matter of choice. I am basically a finger gripper. The club runs along the base of my fingers in both hands. With my short fingers and intermesh grip, this works best for me. It feels powerful and harmonic, as if each hand has an equal 'say' in the grip. The more traditional advice calls for a finger grip in the right hand but a palm-and-finger grip in the left, with the club

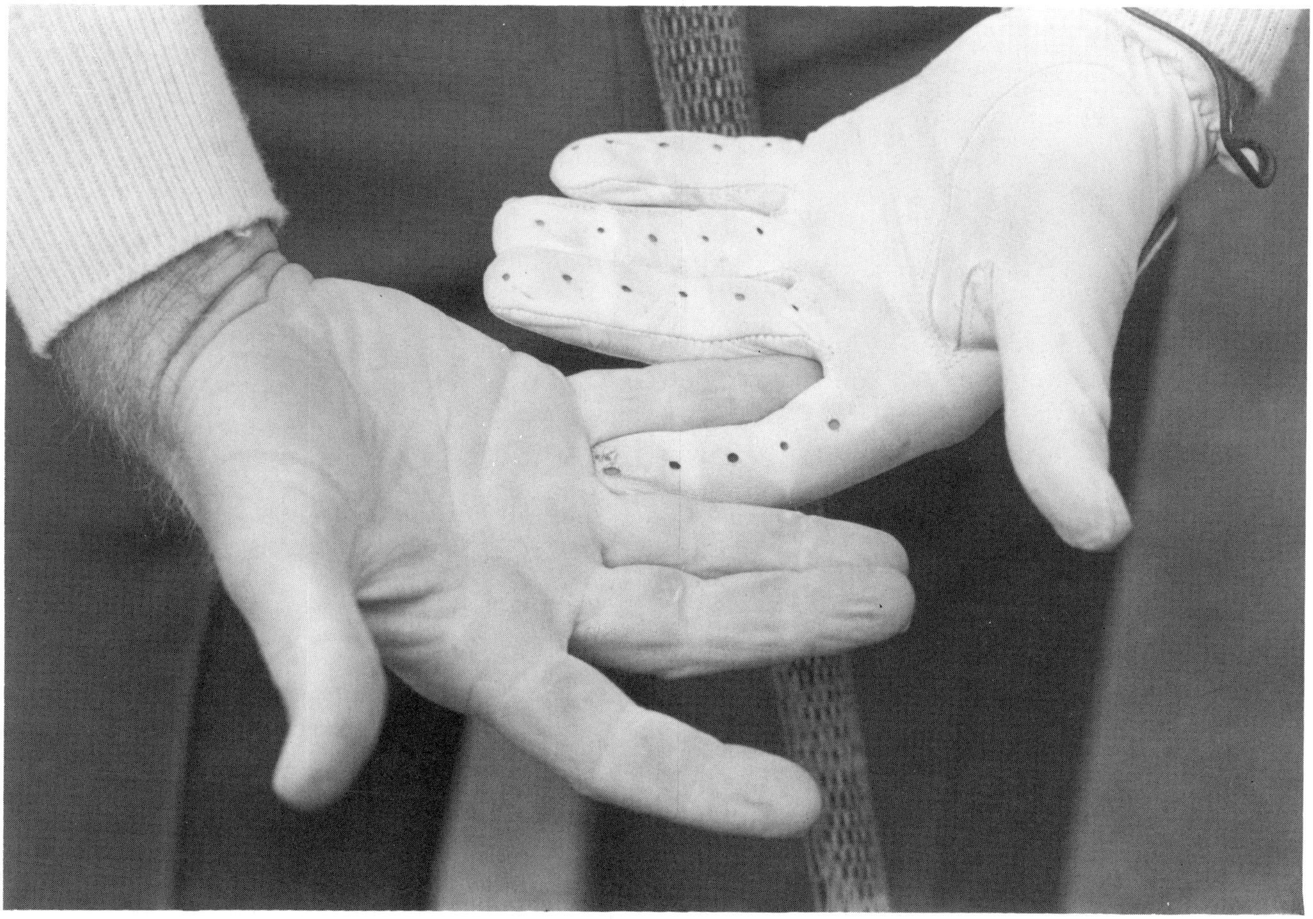

The ten-finger grip puts all the fingers on the club but fails to join the hands together.

In my intermesh grip, the little finger of the right hand fits into the vee between the index and middle fingers of the left hand.

extending on a diagonal line from the base of the index finger to a point just below the meaty pad of the left hand. The thumb of your right hand should rest on the top of the shaft, pointing slightly to the left of the ball, and your left thumb should rest underneath the pad of the right hand and point towards your right foot.

If you have trouble determining whether you have a square grip, take your address position and then look down at your left hand. If between one and two knuckles is visible, you're just about right. If you see no knuckles, you're too weak, and if you see two or more knuckles you're too strong. Another common way to check is to look at the vees formed between the thumbs and forefingers of both hands. If they're pointing to your right ear, you're just about on square. If they're pointing at your chin, you're weak, and if they're at or to the right of your right shoulder, you're strong.

Now let me hasten to add that some very good golfers play with grips that are far from square. In Johnny Miller's grip the vees point almost to the left of his chin, and he has won thirty tournaments including the US and British Opens. Bernhard

Langer plays with an extremely strong grip and he ranks among the finest shotmakers in the game today. But these top-notch professional golfers have the talent and time to make such unorthodox manoeuvres work. Amateur golfers are wiser to adopt a grip that will not tax them.

If your grip is too strong you'll tend to pull your shoulders into a closed position at address, with your left shoulder nearer to the ball than your right. This will result in a flat and wristy swing, and at impact you'll close the clubface across the ball, with a tendency to hit violent hooks. The overly weak grip will tend to pull you into an open stance, with your right shoulder nearer to the ball than your left. This grip will also inhibit your hand and armswing and you'll be less able to make a full, powerful release of the clubhead into the ball. You'll tend to hit weak slices.

The irony is that, for beginners, the strong grip will feel more natural and powerful than a square

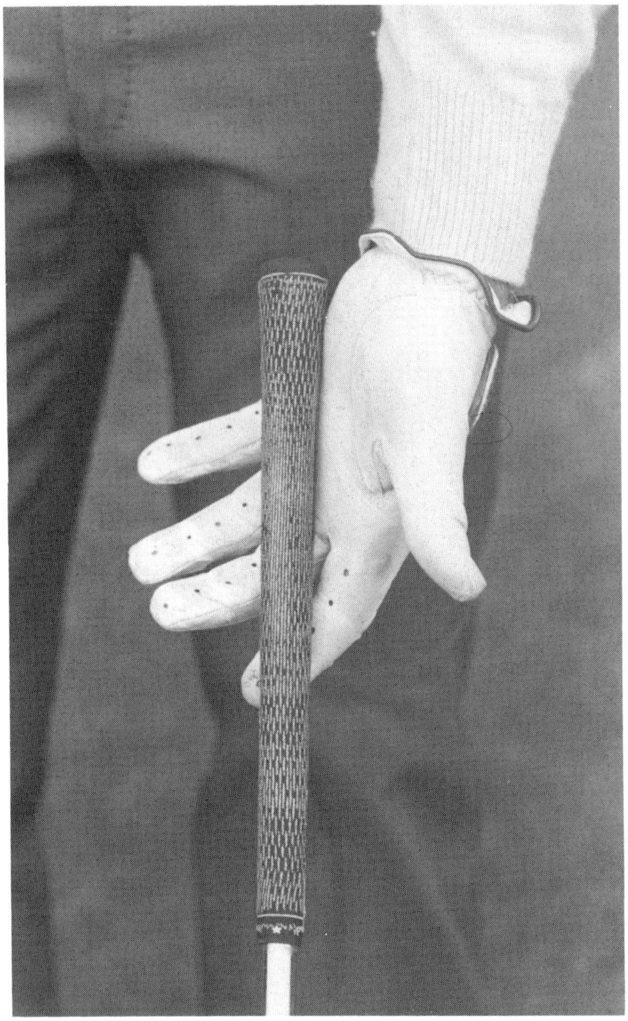

In the left hand the grip extends diagonally, from the base of the index finger to a point just below the pad of the palm.

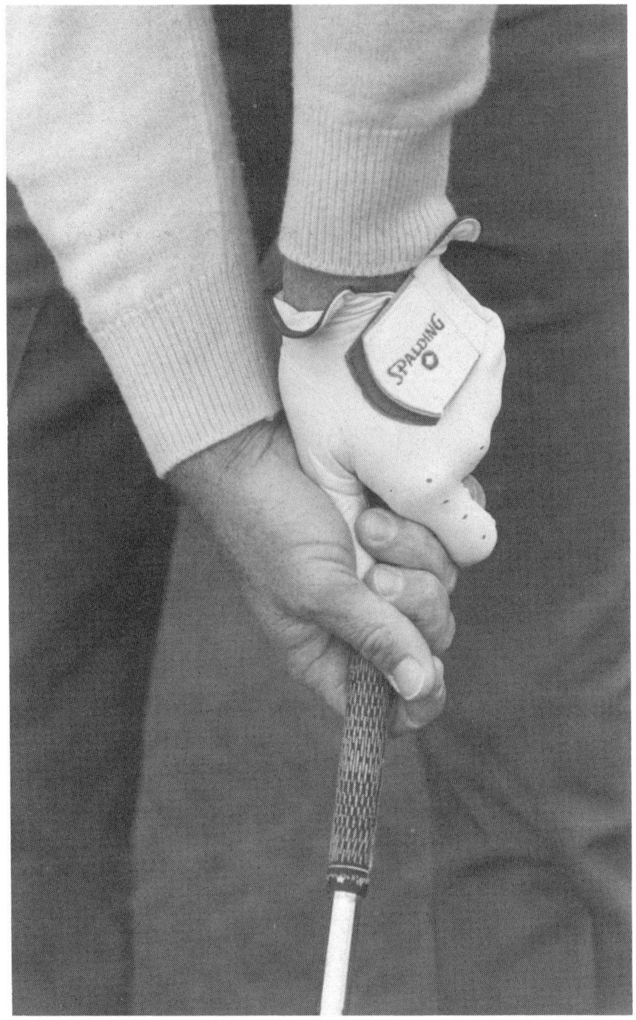

In a strong grip, both hands are turned clockwise on the handle of the club. The vees point to the right shoulder.

grip. But if you're reasonably young and reasonably fit, I urge you to resist the temptation to grip the club in this way. Learn to get your power not from quick, volatile hand action but from the overall strength and solidity of your swing.

I'll make an exception for some women golfers and seniors who have trouble getting adequate distance. In their case, a slightly strong grip will promote a right-to-left draw which will add a few yards of roll to the wood and long-iron shots. As for everyone else, grip the club with your palms parallel and your right palm facing flat at the target.

One more aspect of the grip needs to be discussed – grip pressure. The tension with which you should hold the club is a difficult thing to describe, because 'tight' and 'loose' mean different things to each of us. I feel that when I'm holding the club with the ideal pressure, it's so tight that you couldn't pull it out of my hands unless you yanked very hard

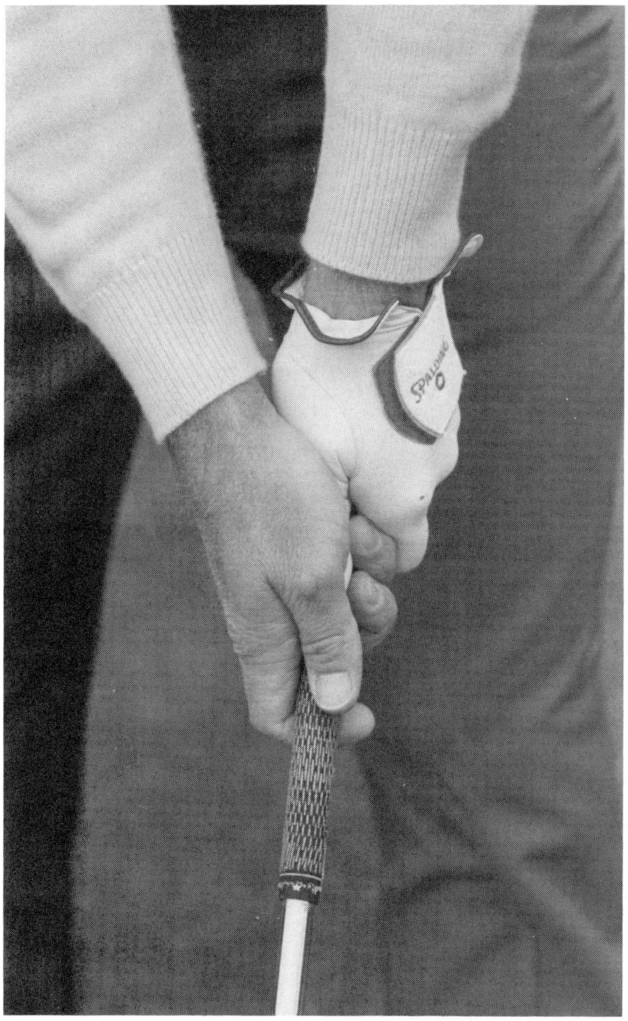

A square grip has the back of the left hand facing the target and the vees pointing at your right ear.

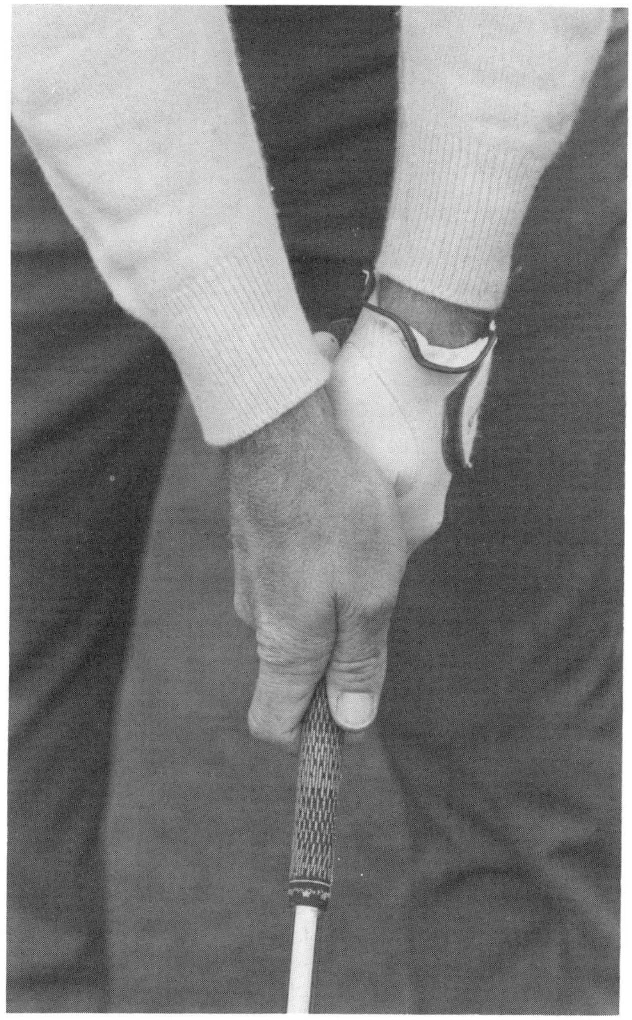

When your hands are turned counterclockwise from the square position, and the vees point at your chin, your grip is weak.

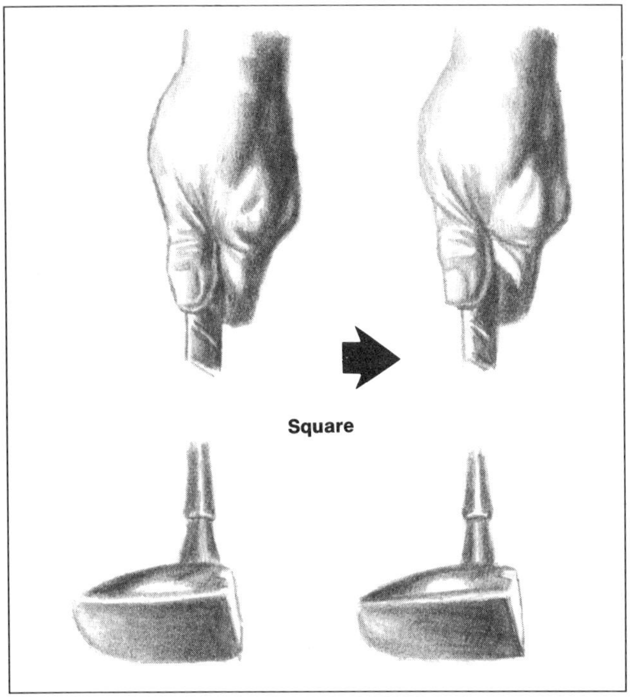

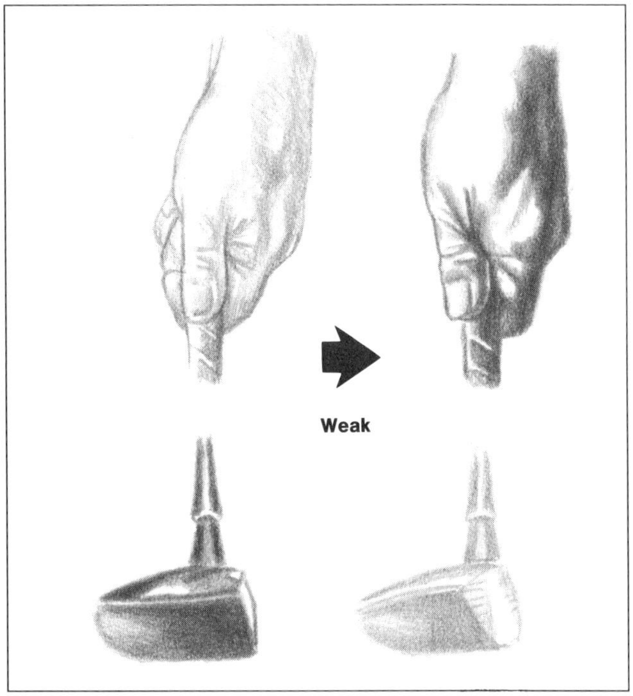

If you hold the club too lightly, you'll tend to lose your grip during the swing, and that leads to all sorts of problems. If you grip it too firmly, you'll tighten your forearms and inhibit the freedom of your armswing. Basically, you need to hold the club tightly enough to keep a secure grip on it and allow the hands to work together as a unit, yet loosely enough to be able to feel the clubhead and allow yourself a free and natural swing that will return the club squarely to the ball.

I tend to grip a bit more tightly in my left hand than in my right. It seems natural to do that because, as a right-hander, my right side is innately stronger than my left and I therefore need to exert a bit more muscle power with the left hand. Beyond that, one of my swing keys is a long, low extension of my arms as I take the club back from the ball. If I were to let the right hand dominate the takeaway, as I did at one point in my career, I'd find myself picking the club up with that right hand and hitting a lot of quick hooks. But by guiding the takeaway with a firm left hand, I'm able to produce a big, wide arc and lots of controlled power.

Occasionally, however, I overdo it, and that was why Jack wanted to talk to me. When I grip too tightly, I tend to hold on to the club as I come through impact. This inhibits my ability to release through the ball, and occasionally I'll tighten up. Instead of swinging my arms freely through and around and up after impact, I tend to swing out and then straight up. My swing becomes too upright and I tend to push the ball dead right.

Jack is one of the most perceptive swing analysts I know, and he understands my golf swing almost as well as I do. Knowing my tendency to lose the occasional shot to the right, he suggested I loosen up my grip just a hair. By doing so, I protected against this blocking-out action. At Turnberry on Sunday, it worked like a charm.

One method I like to use to ensure the proper amount of left-hand grip pressure is the 'short thumb' technique. Take your normal grip with your left thumb extending down the shaft. Now scrunch up your thumb a half-inch or so. Feel how that increases the tautness of your grip in the last three fingers of your hand. This is exactly where

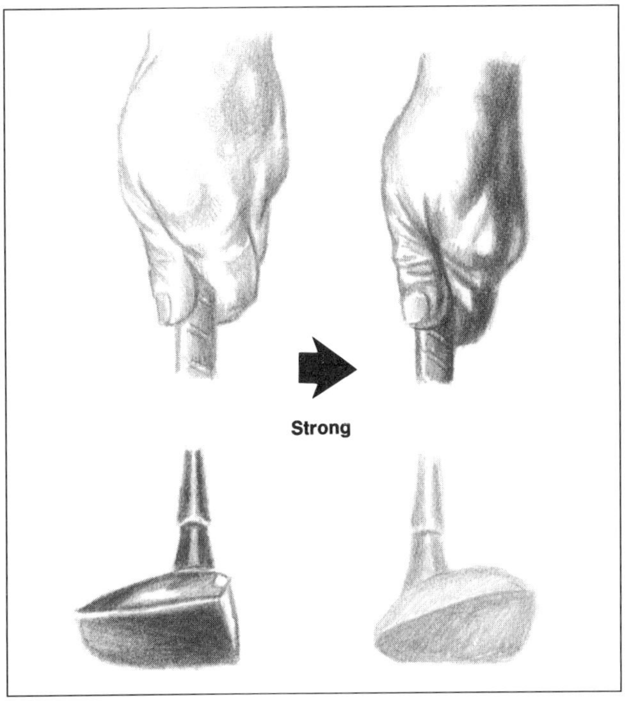

A weak grip leads to an incomplete release, a square grip to a proper release, and a strong grip to an overactive release.

you want to hold the club most securely. One of the first things I check on the practice tee each day is the 'length' of my thumb. When I'm having control problems, it's often because my thumb has lengthened, producing too much looseness at the top of my swing. By shortening the thumb, I automatically induce a crisper, more compact swing. So if inaccuracy is your problem, give the short thumb a try.

Now you know how to assume the proper grip. Almost as important, however, is to know *when* to take your grip. Many amateurs make the mistake of taking the grip too early. They make a practice swing and then just hang on and hit the shot without regripping as they address the ball. Except in the case of putting, that's dead wrong. Other players grip the club too late. Actually they grip and regrip several times during the address procedure, pumping and fidgeting through a series of changes, right up until the second they take the club back. That's not good either.

The proper time to take your grip is at the moment you begin to address the ball. In fact, the taking of the grip is only one part of the more important process of setting your alignment.

Alignment

Of all the things you do before you play a golf shot, setting your alignment is the most important. And certainly it requires the closest attention. After all, for 99 per cent of the shots you play, your grip, posture and overall stance will fall into place. Once you've mastered these things, you don't really have to concentrate on them. But for each and every shot you play you will have a different target requiring careful and precise aim. Good alignment takes work.

Unfortunately, many players fail to realise this. They may think about alignment once or twice

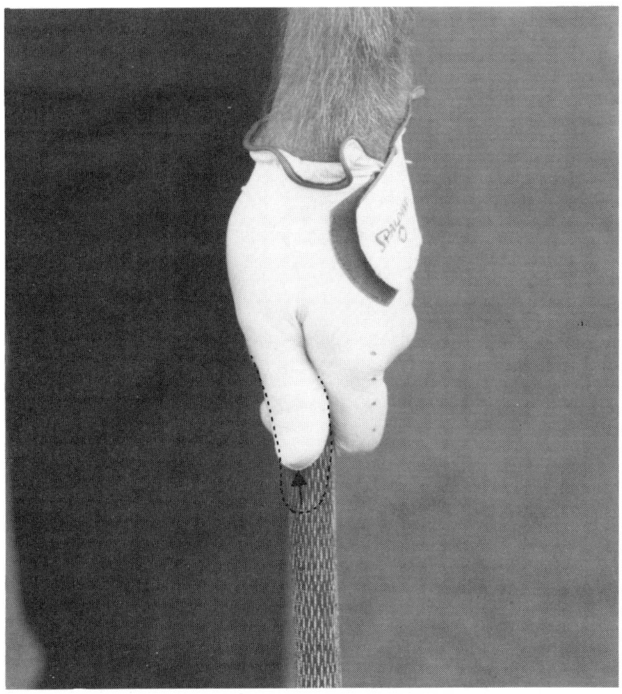

I like to grip with a 'short thumb' because it firms up my hold in the last three fingers of my left hand and thereby induces a crisper, more compact swing.

during a round, but more often they simply swagger into position and swing. Consider what can happen when you're inattentive to your alignment. Remember, you're trying to hit a 1.68-inch-diameter ball a distance of 250 yards or more into a 4.25-inch-diameter hole, with a clubface moving at a speed of 100 miles an hour or so. On a teeshot, an error in alignment of 5 degrees can usually mean a ball in the rough rather than the fairway. An error of 10 degrees may mean a hazard, a lost ball or out of bounds.

Alignment is my number-one priority when I begin to play a golf shot. And because accurate alignment is a demanding and sometimes elusive quality, I try to simplify the aiming process as much as possible. I focus everything on my clubface.

Once I've decided upon the type of shot I want to play, the first move I make is to set my club squarely behind the ball, with the face of the club pointing straight at my target. Holding the club in my right hand only, I approach the ball from behind, sighting up and down that imaginary line that extends from the ball to my target. I then address the ball in a wide-open stance, half-facing the target, still tracking that line from the target to the ball. At this point, I set my club down behind the ball and swivel the clubface minutely back and forth until it's in exact position, pointing dead at the target. Only after this is set do I proceed with the other elements of the grip and address.

I think this clubface method keeps alignment simple. After all, it's far easier to orient yourself to something right next to you than to try to aim at something two or three hundred yards away. Another way I keep things simple is to play virtually all my shots from a square stance.

Once I have my clubface aligned squarely at the target, I simply face my body perpendicular to that clubface. My feet, my knees, my hips and my shoulders all align exactly parallel to that imaginary line that extends from my clubface to the target. Note: I do not align *at* the target because of the fact that I am standing to the side of the ball. I must

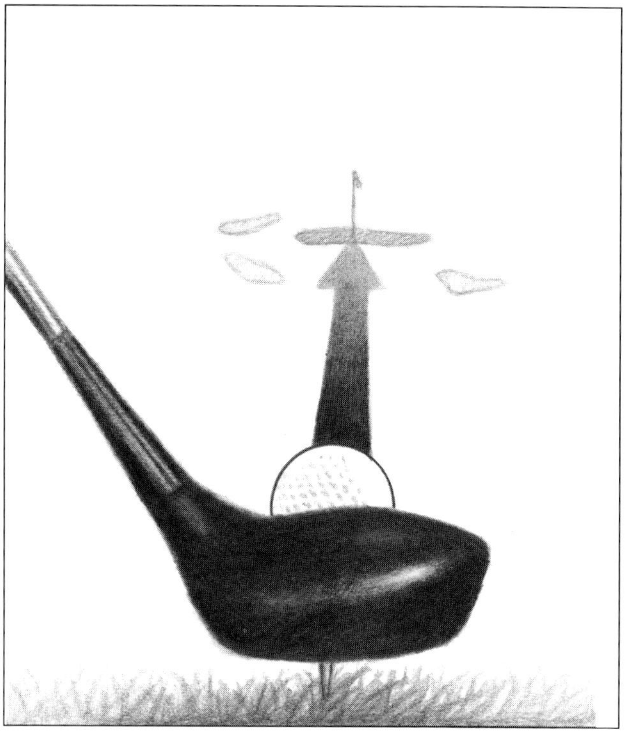

My alignment begins when I set my clubface squarely at my target.

therefore aim at a point just inside the target. This is why I align my body parallel to that clubface-to-target line. The old image of the railroad tracks is a good one, where the outside track is the clubface-to-target line, and the inside track is the line along which you align your body.

Combine this square alignment with a square grip, and you'll make life easy for yourself. You'll eliminate a slew of bad tendencies while giving yourself the best chance of hitting the ball consistently solid and straight.

A closed stance can lead to hooks, pushed and fat shots, an open stance to slices, pulls and topped shots. The fact is, any time you deviate from a square alignment, you create what Ken Venturi calls 'angles', you introduce extra wrinkles and complications in a game that is already sufficiently difficult. The only time to play a full shot with a closed or open stance is when you're in trouble or

One of golf's oldest – and best – images: pretend you're aligning yourself on railroad tracks, with the ball on the far rail and your feet on the near rail.

If you want to check your alignment by setting down a golf club, set it along your heel line, not your toe line.

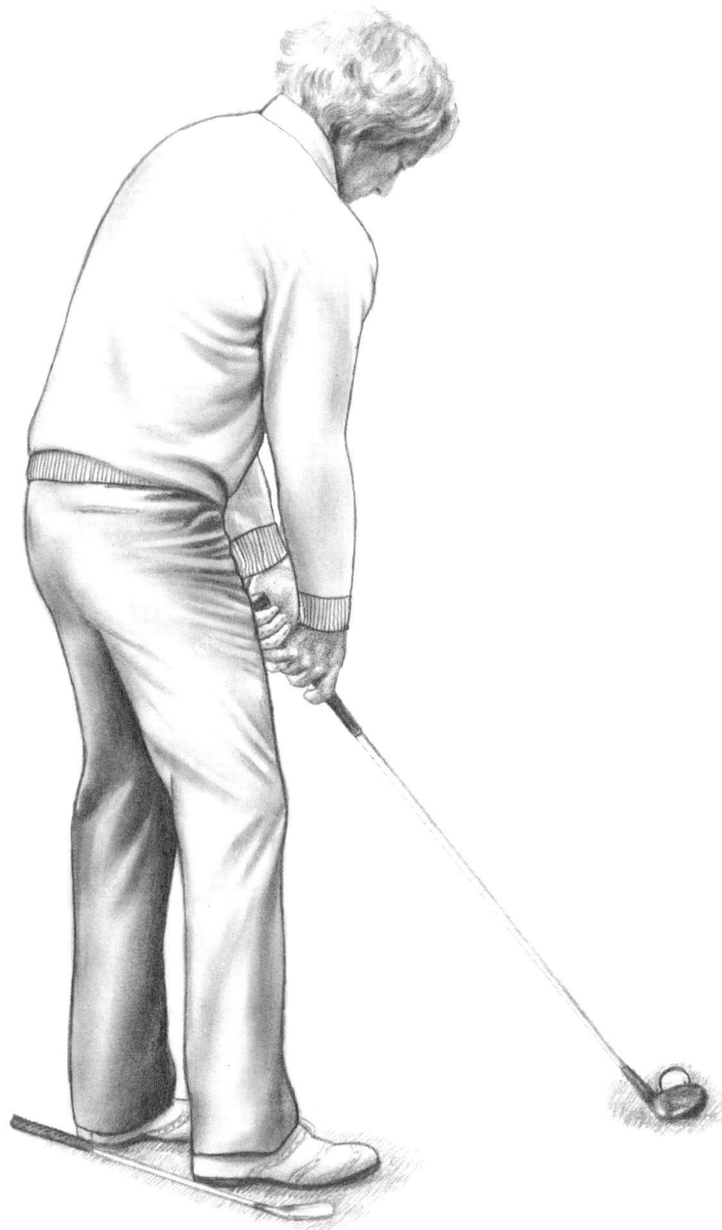

are trying to manoeuvre the ball in some way.

It's a good idea to have a friend or better yet PGA professional check your alignment from time to time. Often your stance can look and feel square to you but your hips and shoulders will be several degrees off-line.

There's also a good way of checking yourself on the practice range. Take your address and align yourself at an easily identifiable object. Then, without moving your feet, take your club and set it down on the ground at the back of your heels. Step away and see whether it's pointing on a line parallel to your target line. If it isn't, set the club on the proper line and leave it there, then go back and take the correct alignment and get used to the look and feel of the proper position.

Traditional instruction suggests you set a club down along your toe line to check alignment. But I don't agree with that for the simple reason that I flare out my left toe slightly at address (more on that later). This brings the toe back slightly from that parallel alignment. If I were to lay a club down on my toe line, it would appear that I was aimed left when the fact is I'm square. So to avoid such confusion, I feel it's wiser – for everyone – to lay the club down along the heels.

Ball Position

If alignment is the most important factor in determining the path of your shots, the second most important is unquestionably ball position. Here again, I recommend that you keep things simple, as I do, and use the same ball position for virtually all full shots.

Some players and teachers advocate playing the ball progressively farther back in your stance, the shorter the club in your hand. But I disagree. If you keep the ball in the same spot for every club, you're going to create one of the most important assets a golfer can have – consistency. When you move the ball back for the shorter clubs, you're basically changing the loft of the club. If, for instance, you play the 6-iron a half-inch farther forward than you do the 7-iron, then what you're doing is taking some of the loft off the 7-iron. In effect, the 7-iron becomes a short 6-iron. Changing ball position changes the point in your swing at which you make contact with the ball. As far as I'm concerned, it's hard enough to worry about one impact point without having to keep track of a dozen of them.

For the vast majority of my full swings, I position the ball at a point just behind my left heel. Through years of trial and error, I've learned that this is the position that works best for me.

Back in 1985 I was having some trouble with my game, and I couldn't figure out my problem. My swing felt fine, but my shots were spraying all over the place. It wasn't until the Dunhill Cup at St Andrews that autumn that I learned what I was doing wrong. My countryman and good friend, Bruce Devlin, who knows my swing well, was doing television commentary on the tournament and spotted my error right away.

He saw that I had allowed my ball position to drift about an inch forward, so that I was playing everything off my left instep. After he told me I went directly to the practice tee. Twenty shots later, I had it completely straightened out. The next day I made eight birdies and tied the course record for the Old Course at St Andrews. That started the finest period of my career. In the following thirteen months I won ten events worldwide.

Ever since that experience I've kept close tabs on my ball position. I now check it every day. In fact, I have a method that allows me to check my alignment and my ball position at the same time. I have a 'picture' I look for at address when I look down through my hands to the club and ball. I know I'm in correct alignment and my ball position is in its proper place when I see the back of the thumb pad of my left hand cover the instep of my left foot. When I don't see this picture, I check my alignment and ball position to determine which of them is off. Once I have that thumb pad eclipsing my left instep I'm back in the groove. And since I play everything from a square stance and with the same ball position, this picture works, no matter what club I have in my hand.

Should you adopt this same position, and this same ideal picture? Probably not. There's quite a range of acceptable ball positions – you could probably play the ball at least one ball-width in front of where I do and at least two ball-widths farther back. Ideally, however, your ball position should be at the very bottom of your swing arc, and that point is different with every physique.

A short, stout person has a relatively low centre of gravity, a flattish swing and a shallow, short arc. He'll tend to reach his swing bottom 'earlier'. He should therefore use a rearward ball position, whereas a tall, lanky person with a higher centre of gravity and a big wide arc will tend to need a more forward ball position, to compensate for the necessary lateral movement in his swing.

Beyond these considerations, a player with a lot of leg action, such as Lee Trevino, will tend to play the ball forward and 'go after it' in his forward swing, whereas a player such as Arnold Palmer, who keeps a very steady swing centre and gets most of his power from a big turn of the upper body, will play the ball back towards the centre of his stance and 'trap it'.

My best advice is to find your ideal ball position just as I did – by trial and error. Then memorise that 'picture' that you see at address when you're playing well, and be able to recreate it before you pull the trigger on any shot.

The Stance

If you have a solid grip, accurate alignment and the proper ball position, most of your pre-swing battle is won. Still, it's important to know the basics of the rest of the address position.

Let's begin at the bottom, with the width of the stance. To me, this is a matter of comfort and common sense. Even if you've never played golf before, you have some idea of the proper width of stance. If your stance is too narrow you won't have enough stability and balance to make a full, wide swing away from the ball. Thus you'll rob yourself of some power. On the other hand, if your stance is too wide, you'll inhibit your ability to make a good shoulder turn, and you'll lose power that way too. The standard rule is that for the driver the width of stance should be about the same as the width of the shoulders. I guess that's a good starting point, but I think you should also have some latitude for personal comfort and preference.

As the length of the club in your hand shortens, the width of your stance should become narrower. Keep that ball position constant, but move your right foot progressively closer and closer to your left foot as you address the fairway woods, long irons, middle irons and short irons, down to a point where, on the wedges, your feet are probably no more than six inches apart. This narrowing of the stance enables you to adjust your swing automatically to the decreased shaft length of the shorter clubs without making any change in your ball position or, for that matter, your swing itself.

With the short irons – the 8-iron through the wedges – I make one additional adjustment. I open up my stance just a few degrees, by pulling my left foot back an inch or so from that square-alignment line. This move encourages a more outward and upward takeaway of the club which results in the slightly more downward attack on the ball that the short irons require.

For all shots, my right foot points perpendicular to the target line, but, as I mentioned earlier, my left toe flares out to the left a bit. This flaring is common practice among better players. One of the first to use it was Ben Hogan, who found it helped him to clear his hips to the left on the downswing.

You should feel free to experiment with the angling of both feet. If you're not particularly flexible and need help in making a backswing turn, you might want to square up your left foot and flare out your right foot a bit. Just be aware that this position will inhibit your ability to turn your hips out of the way on the forwardswing, and you may risk releasing the club too early and snap-hooking the ball. These foot positions are refinements to work on

Ball position remains the same throughout my clubs, but my stance narrows as my right foot moves closer to my left. On the short irons, the stance also opens a bit.

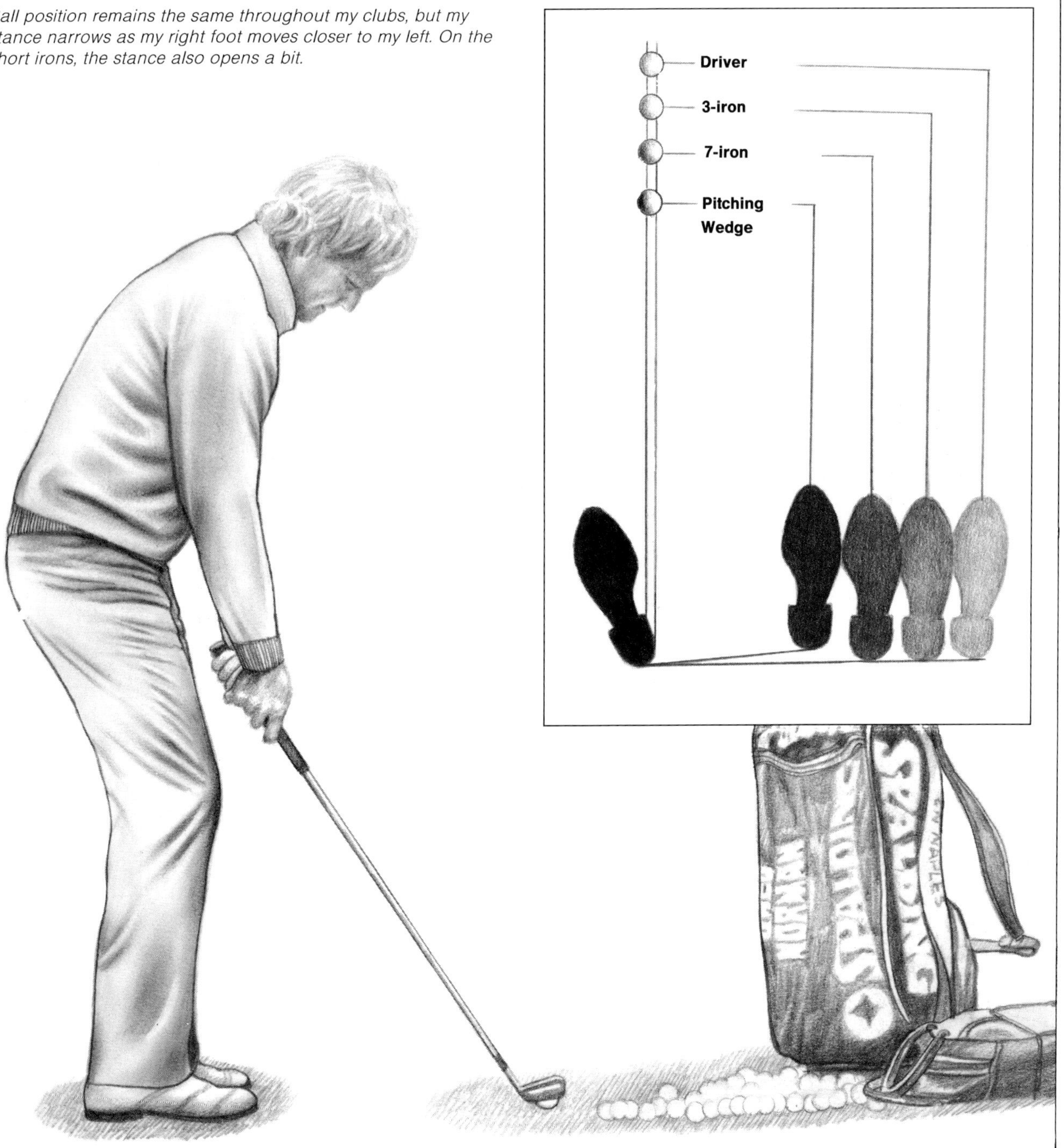

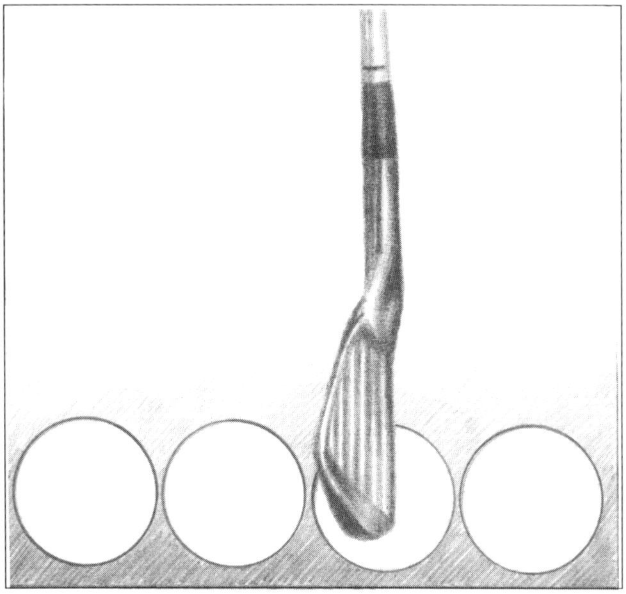

I play the ball just behind my heel for most shots, but you may vary. Up to a ball-width farther forward or two balls back can work, depending on your physique and swing style.

once you've mastered the basic address.

When addressing all full shots, I try to keep my weight balanced about 50–50 between my left and right feet. If you put too much weight on your left side, you'll be susceptible to what's called a reverse weight shift. Instead of transferring your weight from your left to your right side on the backswing, you'll tend to keep your weight left; then on the downswing, instead of moving your weight from right to left, you'll tend to fall back and to the right. The result is a weak impact, usually a slice or pushed shot. On the other hand, if at address you lean too much to the right, you'll tend to snatch the club to the inside, inducing a flat, spinning type of swing that produces smothered shots and hooks. So try to keep your weight evenly distributed.

Within each foot, I put most of my weight on my heel and towards the inside of the foot, in order to maintain good balance and protect against a sway. I occasionally have a bad tendency to let my left knee drift laterally to the right during the backswing, and that leads me to make more of a sway than a proper turn. To guard against that, I make a special effort to pre-set my weight on the inside of my left foot. I do this by angling my left knee slightly to the right at address. By pre-setting my static weight I prevent myself from moving this weight actively during the swing, when the momentum of such a move could create the sway.

Many golfers like to angle in the right knee for much the same reason, to use it as a brace, a sort of gatepost around which the body can turn, rather than allowing it to sway laterally. Ben Crenshaw, in his early days as a professional, had a tendency to lose control of his swing because of this sliding knee. In general it's best to think of your knees as being comfortably flexed and ready to help you rotate your body.

Posture

Now in order to rotate properly, that upper body also has to be in good position, and this is where posture is important. To understand proper posture, let's go back to that 'clapping' position at the beginning of this chapter. Take your flexed-kneed stance, bend slightly from the waist – about 30 degrees – and let your arms hang down naturally. For a player of average height and with standard-length golf clubs, good posture is as simple as this. In this position, your hands should be hanging at exactly the height at which you should grip the club.

Taller players will have to bend a bit more from the waist, to get their hands down to the ball. With these lower hands, they will thus tend to pick the club up a bit more vertically than normal and make a rather upright swing. Shorter players will not need to bend much at address. They'll tend to be higher-handed and swing a bit more flatly, around the body rather than upwards. Basically, your posture should give you three things: stability, flexibility and comfort.

When you've settled into your final address position – grip, alignment, ball position, stance and posture are all set – be sure of two final checkpoints.

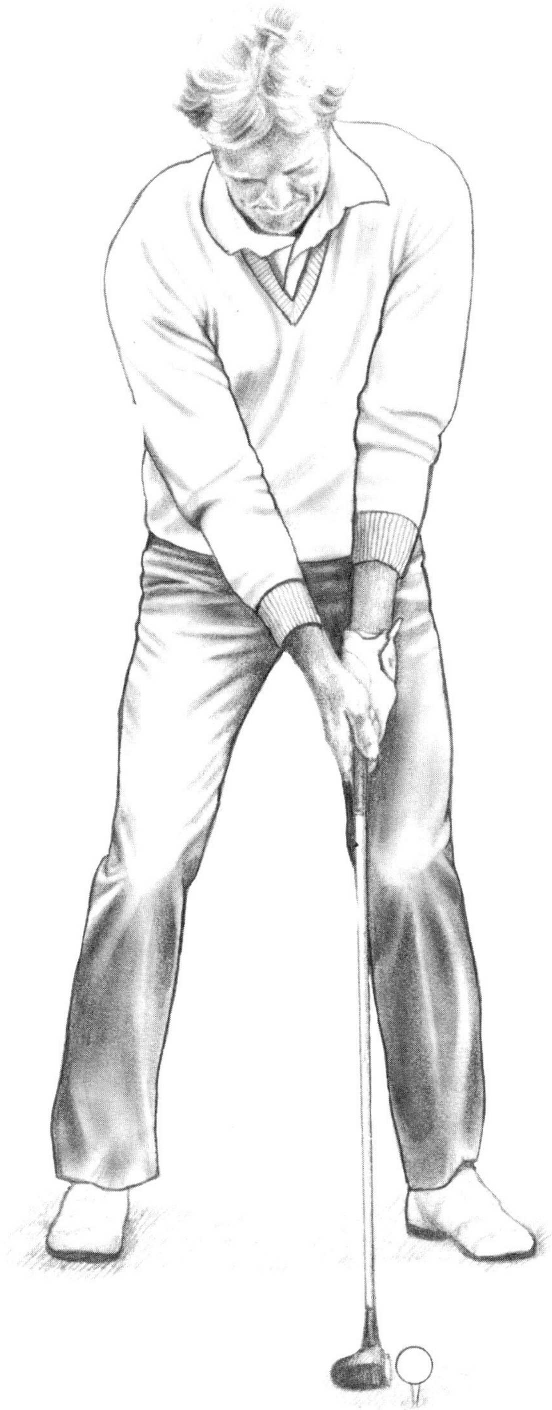

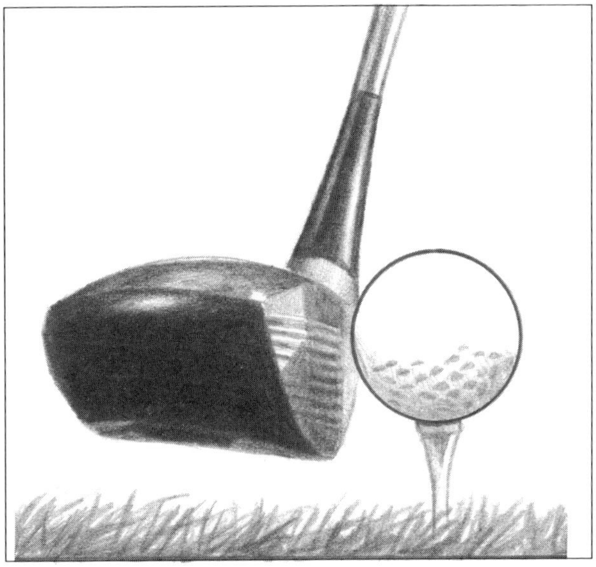

To guard against a quick, snatching takeaway, I hover the driver off the ground before taking it away.

In the proper final address position, the left shoulder is higher than the right and the left arm is in a strong position, virtually a straight extension of the clubshaft.

First, your left shoulder will be slightly higher than your right. The obvious reason for this is that your right hand is lower on the club than your left, so do not try to level up the shoulders. Secondly, your left side should be in a strong and solid position; a straight line should extend from the centre of your left shoulder, down your left arm, through your grip to the clubhead. If your hands are markedly ahead of or behind the clubhead, you're not ready to make a good swing.

Countdown

I've discussed a dozen different positions, checkpoints and movements in this chapter, and it may seem to you that these basics are a bit involved. Well, take heart, you now know as much about the pre-swing fundamentals as anyone needs to know to play top-flight golf. And with a little practice these basics will become second nature. They'll blend together in a smoothly flowing continuum each time you address a shot.

It's important, however, to develop this continuum, this routine to follow on each shot. The way you assume your address sets your rhythm and focuses your mind on the objective of your shot. I mentioned part of my own pattern of address when I discussed the grip. Now, I'd like to walk you through the whole routine. Don't feel you have to adopt this exact order of doing things, but *do* develop something similar, and then adhere to it on every shot you play.

The proper 'countdown' involves both mental and physical steps, and for me it begins about ten feet behind the ball.

1. Having inspected my lie, decided on the shot I want to play and selected my club, I stand back and have a good look at what's ahead of me. At this moment, I visualise the precise shot I want to play. I see the ball leaving my clubface, arching into the sky and coming down next to the target. If it's a teeshot, I may see the ball rolling after impact; if it's an iron, I may see it checking up or spinning back, depending on the nature of my lie. But, quite frankly, these final frames of my mental movie are comparatively unimportant. Contrary to what most people do – visualise the ball coming to rest near their ultimate target – I prefer to focus on the *apex* of the shot in flight.

I prefer this method for a couple of reasons. First, except on two-foot putts, I don't actually hit the ball straight to the target. I'm always playing the break, or allowing for the wind, or expecting some fade or draw or bounce or roll. If my mind is on the target, I'm not giving proper attention to those factors. Indeed, if I become target-fixated, I might tend to start my shot straight at the flag, only to see it blow or drift off course. What I want to do is make my ball reach the very height of its ideal flight, or, in the case of a draw or fade, the farthest right or left point of its curve. This after all is as much as I *can* do – I can't bring it to earth. If I hit the shot with the proper trajectory and shape, gravity and ballistics will do the rest. So I try to get a vivid picture of the spot in the sky where the ball will ultimately reach. (I do this even on putts – I 'see' the ball at the very crest of its break; then I try to hit it there.)

2. With the ideal picture in mind, I walk to the ball and, holding the club with my right hand only, I set the clubhead down on the ground behind the ball. This is where I take careful aim. Standing well open so that I can see the route to the target clearly, I adjust the orientation of the clubface until I've got it pointed straight where I want to go.

3. Now that my aim is set, I begin to align my body and take my grip. I do this by moving my left foot into position, simultaneously setting my left-hand grip on the club. For the next couple of seconds, I get comfortable, shifting my feet and hands until I know my grip is square and secure and my body alignment is in sync with the clubface.

At this point also, I lift the clubhead off the ground, and I keep it off the ground through the rest of my address. You've probably noticed that Jack Nicklaus does the same thing. In fact, it was by reading his book that I adopted this technique. It has a couple of benefits over the alternative,

When planning the ideal shot, I focus on the apex – the highest point to which I want to propel the ball.

grounding the club. First, it establishes the proper grip pressure. The weight of the clubhead forces you to hold the club with a certain amount of tension. It also makes you arch your wrists slightly, a nice way of guarding against letting your hands take over the swing.

Secondly, when you keep the club off the ground there is no chance that you'll get it caught in heavy grass as you swing it away from the ball. You guarantee yourself a smooth, unbroken takeaway. Finally, you lessen the risk of accidentally moving the ball, or of grounding your club in a hazard. Either of these Rules violations would cost you a one-stroke penalty.

4. Once my grip and stance are set, I could immediately swing, but each of us needs a certain amount of time to get comfortable. It's at this point that I take a couple of waggles, quick back-and-forth flexes of the clubshaft, to get loose, get the feel of the clubhead, and home my mind in one last time

Holding the club in my right hand only, I carefully align the face in the direction in which I want to hit.

Once the club is in position, I align my body and take my grip.

on the type of shot I want to play. At some point during the waggling I'll take one last look at the target. Then I'm ready to go.

5. Of course, each of us needs some way in which to pull the trigger. For Gary Player, it's a forward kicking-in of his right knee. For Jack Nicklaus it's the swivelling of his head to the right. It's their way of igniting the swing. My method is unique, at least I've never seen anyone else use it. Throughout the final stages of address sequence, I hover the club just inside the ball. In a sense, I address the ball only with the toe of the clubhead. Many people know that this is the way I address my putts, but the fact is I use the same method on every other shot as well. Just before I begin my swing, however, I slide the clubhead away from me slightly so that it's squarely behind the ball. Fuzzy Zoeller makes the same move, only he starts the club outside the ball and slides it towards him.

Each player has a different swing trigger. Indeed,

A couple of waggles relieve tension and enable me to fine-tune my final address position and focus my concentration.

With all systems 'go', I begin my takeaway.

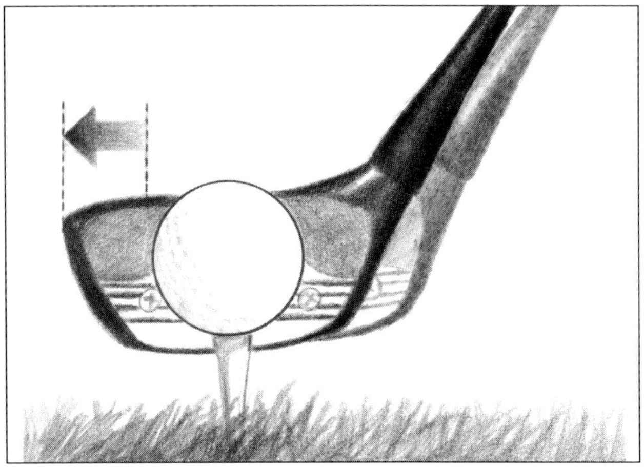

I trigger my swing by sliding my hands outwards a bit so that the ball, formerly positioned off the toe of my driver, is squarely behind the centre of the insert, ready to be swung back.

each of us has a different address countdown, suited to the pace with which he or she does things. Fast players such as Lee Trevino and Lanny Wadkins take very little time in playing their shots. A more deliberate player such as Jack Nicklaus will spend more time over the ball. Personally, I'm a firm believer in making the address countdown as brief as possible. For one thing, it's good etiquette and moves the game along a bit faster. But more important, a brisk pace helps breed confidence. One fault many players get into is the incessant fiddling and fidgeting during the address. It seems to me that they're second-guessing themselves at a time when they should be absolutely confident and ready to swing. US Open and PGA Champion Hubert Green went through a period when he pumped his grip up to twenty times before finally taking the club back, and that was when he played some of his worst golf. After he cut his address routine in half, he doubled his productivity as a player. It doesn't take long to get comfortably aligned. Trevino and Wadkins, two of the game's most accurate players, are also two of its fastest players.

No matter what the duration of your pre-swing routine, the most important point is that you stick with that routine and use it on every shot. Don't let outside interferences interrupt your countdown either. If a car horn honks while you're setting your stance, step back. Step *all the way back.* On occasion, I've gone as far as to put the club back into the bag and then take it out again – the same club – just so I could 'take it from the top' and regain my rhythm and confidence.

After you've developed your routine, you'll be surprised at how dependent on it you'll become. I'll never forget the strange feeling I had during the third round of the British Open at Turnberry. A howling rainstorm hit when I was in the middle of the 17th fairway. I mean, that rain was coming horizontally!

The difficulty, however, was not so much in swinging in this rain as it was in getting ready to swing. I simply couldn't use my normal routine. I'd get out there, holding the club in my right hand only and trying to align the face, and the rain would soak the grip, so that by the time I tried to grip the club, the leather was too slippery to hold. After trying two or three times to keep to the routine, I gave up and improvised, taking my grip under my umbrella, then walking to the ball, waggling a couple of times, and hitting. Fortunately, I got through the storm relatively unscathed. But it was the discomfort of being without my routine that bothered me more than the rain.

Thank goodness, such conditions are rare. So learn these basics, and put them all together in a brisk, efficient countdown, and you'll have the solid foundation to play your aggressive best.

Me with daughter Morgan-Leigh at the Suntory World Match Play, 1986.

Winning the British Open in 1986 at Turnberry, Ayrshire.

Chipping into the green at the AT & T National Pro-Am in 1987. On a chip shot your heels should be no more than six to eight inches apart.

Coming out of the rough, British Open, 1986.

Hitting the ball out of the rough at the 1984 Dunlop Masters.

Arnold Palmer, Jack Nicklaus, Raymond Floyd and me at the Shark Shootout Charity Match, 1986.

The US Open, 1987, after hitting the ball off the tee.

In the World Series, 1986.

Left. *Contemplating my next shot on the green at the British Open, 1986.*

Acknowledging the crowd during the British Open, 1986.

Right. *Hitting out of the bunker at the 18th green during the Australian Masters, Melbourne, 1987.*

If you are in the rough, you may have a flyer lie. The first thing to remember is to use less club than you would for a fairway shot of the same distance. US Masters, 1987.

Left. *Again coming out of the bunker, this time at the American Masters in 1983.*

Playing in the 1987 US Masters.

Me with the National Panasonic New South Wales Open Trophy, which I won for the fourth time in Sydney in 1986.

Dunhill Cup, 1986: Rodger Davis, me and David Graham.

CHAPTER 3

Taking Control of the Hole

THE DRIVER SWING

During a practice round for the 1984 British Open at St Andrews I gave the 18th-hole spectators – and myself – a thrill when I hit my teeshot the length of the 354-yard hole on to the green. From there I two-putted for an easy birdie. As I was leaving the green, a little old Scottish gentleman in the gallery tapped me on the arm.

'I can see, laddie,' he said, 'that you've discovered the key to great golf.'

'What's that?' said I.

With a twinkle in his eye, he replied, 'Eliminate the second shot.'

I wish it were that easy. Unfortunately, I'm seldom able to drive par-fours, particularly on the long, lush courses of America. Still, on most of the holes I play, my goal is to hit my first shot as far and as straight down the fairway as possible.

Don't ever try to sell me on that line, 'Drive for show and putt for dough.' If you can't put your teeshot in play, the smoothest stroke in the world won't help you. To my mind, the most important shot in golf is the drive. Hit it well, and you have a jump on the hole, an edge on your opponent. Hit it poorly, and you'll struggle all the way to the green.

However, as befits the most important shot, the long, straight drive is also the most difficult shot in golf. After all, it's the only swing where you're trying to maximise both distance and accuracy. Heck, I could hit every fairway if I wanted to tee-off with a 3-iron, but that would advance me only 200 yards towards the hole. Besides, it's not in my blood. The challenge – and the joy – for every aggressive golfer is to hit that fairway with the longest club in the bag.

The Basics

The Takeaway

If you've developed a sound set of pre-swing fundamentals, as outlined in Chapter 2, the rest of the game is little more than, as one instructor puts it, 'two turns and a swish'.

I agree entirely with Jack Nicklaus, who believes that the most important part of the swing is the first eighteen inches you move the club away from the ball. The 'takeaway', as it is commonly known, sets the pattern for every motion that will follow it.

'Low and slow' are the key words here. You want to glide the club away from the ball, keeping it as close to the ground as possible for as long as possible. This is the way to establish the wide swing arc that delivers maximum centrifugal force and power. The farther you can extend that clubhead away from your body (while still maintaining good balance and timing) the longer you will hit the ball.

The way to effect this low, slow movement is to start your swing with your entire body. The takeaway may appear to be a movement initiated with the hands only, but you must actually drive it with your hands, arms, shoulders and even your lower body, all working in unison.

If you were to use your hands only, you'd tend to pick the club up in a wristy motion that is neither low nor slow. The sooner you cock your wrists, the shorter arc you'll produce, and the less power you'll put into the drive.

I like to key on my left elbow during the takeaway. I've found that, the farther I can move my left elbow directly away from the target, the longer, stronger takeaway I make. Also, by keying on the elbow, halfway up my arm, I bring everything into play. It's as if the elbow pushes the hands and wrists, and pulls the shoulders. The pushing action eliminates any wristiness, and the pulling ensures that the upper torso begins its backswing rotation.

The feeling I get when making a good takeaway is not unlike the feeling when I bend down and hold my little son Gregory and then swing him gently to and fro. Gregory is about twenty pounds heavier than my driver, so there's no way I can give him a quick, wristy pick-up!

Good overall swing tempo begins with the takeaway. If you snatch the club away quickly, you'll either continue that frantic pace throughout the swing or overcompensate and decelerate on the way to the ball. Either error is devastating. On the other hand, if you take the club back *too* slowly for the first foot and a half, you'll subconsciously feel the need to get things moving faster, and invariably you'll jerk upwards in the backswing, producing more of a lift than a proper turn.

Sometimes I actually watch myself take the club back, even as I'm playing a tournament. I don't really follow the club with my eyes, but I do sort of monitor the movement with my peripheral vision, to be sure I'm gliding it back at the proper speed and in the proper direction.

The path on which the club should travel during the takeaway is a subject of much discussion. A few years ago, I wrote in one of my articles for *Golf* Magazine that the takeaway should be straight back from the ball. Shortly thereafter, I got a letter from an irate reader.

'Have you ever tried to take the club straight back from the ball?' he asked. 'It's impossible!' Well, of course it's impossible, for the simple reason that we stand to the inside of the ball. Eventually, as the hips and shoulders turn, the club will have to begin to travel inwards and around the body. My point in that article, and in this book, is this: if you will make a conscious effort to take the club back straight for as long as possible, you'll give yourself the optimum chance for a powerful, square-faced return of the clubface to the ball.

The Extension

The extreme end of the takeaway – the point when the club stops moving straight back and is ready to start coming inside – is called the extension position. At this stage your swing is irretrievably in motion. You won't be able to stop it or change it or improve it. From this point on, you will be a victim or a beneficiary of the way you have addressed the ball and taken the club away. Nonetheless, it's worth studying the extension position as well as the other stages of the backswing and downswing, in order to understand the positions your swing should achieve along its path away from and back to the ball. Ideally, you should have pictures taken of your swing – either still photographs or better yet with a video cassette recorder, so that you can accurately evaluate your own positions.

In the proper extension, the toe of your clubface should point straight at the sky and the back of your left wrist should be parallel to the target line. At this point, your shoulders have turned about 40 degrees, but your lower body hasn't moved much. Your knees have remained flexed as they were at address, and although the left knee may have moved a hair towards the ball, the right knee remains braced, ready to act as the pivot point for your coiling backswing. From this point, you'll begin the major part of your hip and shoulder turns while swinging the club up and around your back.

As I complete my backswing, I can actually feel the muscles in the upper left part of my back stretching. This is caused by the pull of centrifugal force exerted by the swinging clubhead. At the same time, that force is pulling on my hands and wrists, causing them to cock. By the time I reach my full coil, my shoulders will have turned about 120 degrees and my hips about 60 degrees.

My biggest fault is in not completing those turns. Occasionally, after reaching a good extension position, I'll get lazy and lift the club straight up with my arms rather than continuing to rotate. When that happens, I sway to the right, my backswing becomes too vertical and the result is that I cut across the ball, producing a blocked or sliced shot.

Indeed, the sway is my worst swing enemy, and I've seen it ruin the swings of countless amateurs as

In my takeaway I key on my left elbow. The farther I can move it away from the target, the longer, stronger move I'll make.

Once in this extension position, the swing is on 'go'. You will be a victim or beneficiary of the way you've addressed the ball and taken away the club.

well. Although my sway is basically caused by a laziness with regard to my backswing turn, the more common cause is a faulty weight shift. To guard against this you must try to keep your weight on the insides of your feet.

As you move to the top of your backswing you should feel most of your weight shifting to the inside of your right foot. If you've maintained the brace in your right knee, you should be able to contain your shift in this way. If, however, you feel your weight drifting to the outside of your foot, you're swaying. A sway will make it virtually impossible for you to return your body and clubhead to their proper positions at impact.

It was this fault that cost me the 1986 Masters. Needing a birdie on the 72nd hole to win, a tie to get into a playoff with Jack Nicklaus, I hit a good drive into the centre of the fairway. But that fairway climbs severely uphill to the green. I was left with an uphill shot of about 187 yards and I decided to

One bad way to make a long swing is by bending the left elbow too much.

Another fault – tiptoeing at the top of the swing.

play a high, soft 4-iron to the back of the green where the pin was positioned.

Now, in order to hit that shot, I had to be sure to keep my weight a bit more behind the ball than usual – that's one way to ensure lots of height. So I made an extra effort to shift my weight to the right on my backswing. In fact, I got too much weight going down that hill. By the time I reached the top of my swing, I knew I was in trouble – I had over-shifted and could feel myself falling backwards down the hill. It wasn't perceptible to anyone watching the shot, but I certainly felt it. The result was a big push, well right of the green, and a bogey that left me as joint runner-up with Tom Kite.

The correct top-of-swing, with the hips and shoulders coiled powerfully around a braced right leg.

The Top of the Swing

If you want to make solid contact at the bottom of your swing, you must have absolutely solid control of the club at the top. And 'control' has nothing to do with the length of your backswing. I don't care whether you take a three-quarter swing or the club goes 30 degrees past parallel. It's the *way* you get to the top of your swing that's important.

The object on the drive is to make the biggest *good* swing you can. Unfortunately, many players make big bad swings. One common mistake is to let go of the club at the top, loosening the hold with the fingers. I've noticed that this is a prevalent problem among people who grip too tightly at address. By the time they get to the top, their hands are unable to maintain the pressure, so they let go. There's little hope for a regrip and recovery from this error. Another bad way to a long swing is to make a big bend in the left elbow. This one's a real cheater's method – it can get the club way past parallel, but it introduces an extra hinge in the middle of the armswing, and that hinge rarely works smoothly. Finally, there's the 'tiptoe' overswing, where the player comes up on his left toe, lurches to his right and reaches for the sky. It may feel powerful, but it looks terrible, and from this position at the top you'll need a team of sherpa guides to get you safely back to the ball.

The right way to achieve a maximum backswing is to coil the hips and shoulders around the right knee while retaining a firm hold on the club. Keep your grasp, particularly in the last three fingers of the left hand. You may allow a tiny bit of left-elbow bend, but the key word is 'allow'. Don't try to bend the elbow, simply let it flex as the centrifugal force of the swinging clubhead pulls on your hands and arms. As far as raising the left heel is concerned, I never raise mine, but I admit that I'm very supple.

Some excellent players – Jack Nicklaus and Tom Watson among them – allow their left heels to come off the ground at the top of the swing. I'd say this is all right if you're thickly built through the upper torso and have trouble making a full pivot. But if you can avoid it, please do.

A full backswing depends mostly on your ability to turn away from the ball. Try to turn your hips and shoulders so that, at the end of your swing, your back faces the target. That's a turn of almost 100 degrees – all you need to hit a powerful teeshot. If you can't turn that far, the best thing to do is to work on your flexibility. Stretching exercises will help, as will practice swings with a heavily weighted club. Just don't try to 'cheat' your way to a bigger turn – it won't work.

But a good top-of-swing position involves more than just the length the clubshaft has travelled. That shaft also has to be pointing in the proper direction. When you're in good position, the back of your left wrist should be flat, and the club should point exactly parallel to the target line. In this position, the clubface is square – pointing roughly on a 45-degree angle towards the sky.

Golfers with overly flat swings tend to get the left wrist into a bowed position at the top with the clubshaft pointing well to the left of the target and the clubface in a closed position, pointed almost straight up into the sky. Even talented players such as Arnold Palmer and Lee Trevino exhibit this position. But Trevino makes a strong lateral move with his legs in the downswing, and Palmer simply muscles the ball with his powerful upper body, and each of those movements helps to get the club back on track by impact. Most amateur players who get into the flat position at the top lack the athletic ability to make such moves. As a result, they either smother the ball or hook it violently.

The other faulty top-of-swing position is the overly upright swing that produces a cupped wrist, a shaft that points to the right of the target and a clubface that is aligned almost vertical with the ground. Again, some good players get into this position, particularly the younger pros such as Corey Pavin and Fred Couples. This type of swing can produce lots of distance because it takes the clubhead on a long trip away from the ball. Check the length of Pavin's backswing for example. That clubhead almost hits him in the left hip! But Corey and Fred have the strength and flexibility to turn their hips actively on the downswing and re-flatten their planes in time for a solid impact. Again, this cupped position is not recommended for most players.

Check your position in photos or videotape of your swing, or in a mirror, or just ask a friend to tell you what you look like at the top. Basically, you're in good shape if your hands swing to a point just above the tip of your right shoulder. If they're outside or below your shoulder you're too flat and if they're between your shoulder and your neck, you're too upright.

If you find that you're too flat or upright at the top of the swing, go back to your address and takeaway and try to find the reason. You may be standing closed or open, your grip may be too strong or weak, your takeaway may be too much to the inside or outside. Experiment a bit with your pre-swing basics and takeaway, and see what effects these adjustments have on your top-of-swing position. When you start swinging the club into the proper slot, adopt those adjustments, and ingrain that move. This type of self-diagnosis, followed by trial and error, is the very essence of aggressive golf – doggedly pursuing a higher level of play.

The Downswing

I've always found it helpful to think of the golf swing as a horse race among the various body parts. Every 'horse' leaves the starting gate at the same time, in a unified takeaway, and everyone hits the finish line simultaneously in a mass photo finish, but in between the field spreads out a bit.

The first horses to reach the top of the backswing are the knees and hips, followed by the shoulders which have had to rotate twice as far. After the shoulders complete their rotation, the arms go a bit farther and then stop before the wrists complete their cocking as the weight of the clubhead gives a final downward tug.

It's the same leaders on the way down to impact. Even as the wrists are completing their part of the turn, the lower body has moved into the back-stretch of the race. The left knee moves laterally into the forwardswing and pulls on the left hip which in turn pulls the left arm downwards. At the same time, the right knee begins to drive towards the target, taking with it the shoulders, arms and hands.

At the last split-second before impact the race tightens again, as the swiftly moving arms catch up with the bigger muscles in the shoulders, hips and legs. When you execute the swing properly, the leadership of the legs creates a lag of the hands and clubhead, resulting in what's commonly called a delayed release. In this position, just prior to impact, the wrists have not yet uncocked and there is a tremendous amount of clubhead speed ready to be unleashed. That's what happens in the final millisecond – the club whips through and catches the rest of the body parts, all of which have achieved impact at the same moment. In a good swing, your position at impact is almost identical to your final position at address.

If you've executed the swing correctly, the club will move straight along the line for about a foot on either side of the ball. One good way of encouraging this action is to imagine a second ball about a foot and a half past your actual ball, and then striving to hit that ball in addition to the real one.

Post-Impact

Once past impact there's nothing you can do to influence the flight of the ball, but since a good follow through is the result of a sound swing, it pays to know what the proper finish position looks like.

Basically, you're facing the target. About 80 per cent of your weight has transferred back to your left side. In fact, after impact that weight is for the first time on the outside of your foot, as you roll on to the side of your left foot while balancing on the toe of your right. Your hands, which have been pulled almost violently through impact, now begin to come back inside and upwards, into a final position over your left shoulder. Most important, you're in balance – not tilting back or forward, left or right, but totally stable.

A couple of years ago, one of the trademarks of my swing was a pronounced slide of my right foot towards my left foot just after impact. That happened because I transferred so much of my weight on to my right side on the backswing, then returned so much of it to my left side on the downswing. A swing computer once measured the pros on the US PGA Tour and found that I made the most pronounced weight shift of anyone. Over 90 per cent of my weight was going back and forth during the swing. That 170-pounds of pull simply brought my right foot along with it.

These days, I set up with a slightly wider stance than I used to. In this way, I start with a bit more weight on my right side at address, and therefore I don't have to shift as much during the swing. This minute change has virtually eliminated the slide. It's also had the benefit of counteracting a tendency to hit the occasional errant shot to the right.

The one aspect of the swing I haven't said much about is tempo. That's because I feel it's largely an individual matter and should be matched to your overall temperament and the speed with which you generally do things. If you walk and talk quickly, you should probably swing quickly (although not *too* quickly). If you do things in a more deliberate fashion, then by all means adopt a more leisurely pace of swing.

Just be sure to keep your tempo constant throughout the round. One mistake that all of us have a tendency to make is to speed things up a bit when the pressure is on. I know I do. Back at Turnberry, when I let a couple of shots get away from me and bogeyed the 5th hole of the final round, my caddie, Pete Bender, said to me, 'Slow down – you're swinging fast, you're even walking faster

These next five pages show two views of my driver swing, side-on (top sequence) and front-on (bottom).

If your hands are outside your shoulder, your backswing has been too flat.

If, at the top of the swing, your hands are between your shoulder and your neck, you've made an overly upright swing.

In the proper top-of-swing position, your hands are directly over your right shoulder.

To develop the proper extension through impact, imagine hitting a second ball, about a foot and a half beyond the actual ball.

than normal. I'm going to walk a bit more slowly, and you just keep pace with me.' That put me right back on my natural tempo, and I had no problems from there to the finish.

With regard to your rhythm – the way the backswing and downswing work together – the downswing clearly must be faster-paced than the backswing. But that doesn't mean you should consciously speed up on the way to the ball. Good rhythm and tempo can't really be taught, they must be absorbed. My best advice is for you to go to a Tour event, sit by the practice tee for a while, and watch the pros. Seve Ballesteros is a particularly good model. His marvellous rhythm and tempo never vary, no matter what club he has in his hands.

The Aggressor's Edge

The foregoing discussion of the driver swing will help you to hit your teeshot. But that's not enough. You also need to know how to *play* your teeshot. Hitting your teeshot begins as you take the club back, but playing your teeshot begins at the moment you step up to the hole.

Sadly, most amateur golfers fail to realise this. Without thinking or planning their shot, they walk to the midpoint between the teemarkers, plunk the tee in the ground, and hit. If you're one of these people, you're doing yourself a big disservice. The tee is the only place in golf where you're able to give yourself an absolutely perfect lie. If you don't take full advantage of that edge, you're a fool.

The Teeing Area

The Rules of Golf allow you to tee the ball anywhere between the markers and up to two clublengths behind the markers. This allows you to plan your teeshot so that you can launch the ball from the precise point within that teeing area that offers you the best chance of success.

When I get to the tee of a par-four or five, the first thing I do is ask my caddie, 'Where is the pin today?' Then I play the hole backwards in my mind. If it's a par-four and the pin is on the right side of the green, then the safest and easiest approach to that pin will invariably be from the left side of the fairway. Thus, I'll want to play my drive to that left side, which in turn means that I should tee the ball up on the far *right* side of the teeing area, to give myself the best angle at that landing area. Playing a golf hole in this way is like tacking your ship in a sailing race. It's strategy intended to take advantage of the conditions.

If I'm hitting a teeshot to the right side of the fairway, I'll sometimes go as far as to tee my ball

At the finish, your weight should be on the outside of your left foot, with your right foot perpendicular, toe to the ground.

just inside the left-hand teemarker, and then stand *outside* the teeing ground. This is perfectly legal and it gives you the best possible edge, assuming you can mentally block out that teemarker!

I also move my teeing position according to the hazards on the hole and the way the fairway bends. If, for instance, there's a water hazard on the left side of the fairway, I'll invariably tee up on the right side of the tee, aim *at* that hazard, and play a left-to-right shot that will curve away from the water. When the water (or out of bounds or whatever) is on the right, I'll tee up on the left and play a right-to-left shot to work away from the trouble.

If you're unable to play fades and draws, however, you should consider the opposite strategy. When the worst hazard is on the left, tee up on that side and hit to the right-hand side of the fairway, directly away from the hazard. When the trouble is on the right, tee up on the right and aim your drive to the left. And if you hit all your shots with the same type of flight, clearly you should allow for it on every tee. If, for example, you hit everything with a left-to-right bend, then you should be teeing virtually every drive next to the right-hand teemarker.

On doglegs, I'll adopt the same strategy. If the hole curves to the right, I'll tee my ball on the right side of the teeing area and try to fade the ball from left to right around the corner of the dogleg. When the hole curves from right to left, I'll tee up on the

Beware of teeing areas that are constructed so that they point towards trouble, and be doubly wary of teemarkers that are improperly aligned.

◀Left:
When I want to hit a shot to the right side of a fairway, I'll sometimes 'stretch' the teeing area by teeing the ball just inside the left-hand marker and standing outside the marker. It's perfectly legal.

If you have a sweeping swing, a high tee probably will suit you.

left side and hit a draw that follows the path of the fairway. If I were to try to play that draw from the right side of the tee, I'd risk curving the ball into trouble on the left side. But again, if you're basically a straight-ball hitter, you might want to try the opposite tack. On a left-to-right hole, stand on the left side of the tee, and hit your ball at a point just outside the corner of the dogleg. On the right-to-left hole, stand on the right and hit left for the corner. No matter which way you play it, remember that the idea is to make the golf course play as short as possible. Angling your teeshot aggressively does just that.

Before you put the tee in any part of the teeing area, however, stand back and take a good look at the lie of the land. Many architects, whether out of ignorance or sadism, design tees that point off-line, and some of them actually point into the worst trouble. To compound this, the two teemarkers are often misaligned, one placed well forward of the other, so that the tee box is oriented towards no man's land. So when you get to the tee, step to the rear of it and take a good look.

At the same time, try to pick out the precise spot on the tee that will give you the best lie for your shot. Not simply the right-side/left-side strategy, but the exact patch of grass. If, for instance, you want to play a left-to-right shot, look for any uneven area of the tee which might afford you a lie with the ball a bit below your feet. This lie always

A low tee will be your preference if you make a strong lateral move and hit down and through the ball.

promotes a fade. For a draw, try to find a lie where the ball will be a bit above your feet.

Also, look for an area that will give you firm footing. Most golfers wrongly concern themselves more with the lie of the ball than with the surface under their feet. When the teeing area is wet, sand-based or in scruffy condition, you should seek out a spot that will give you the best stance. It's better to make an aggressive swing at a less-than-perfect lie than an off-balance swing at a perfect lie.

The height at which to tee a drive is something each of us has to work out for ourselves. To a great degree, it depends on your swing. If you're basically a sweeper of the ball, you probably like the feeling of staying under and behind the ball at impact. A rather high tee, with more than half the ball above the driver at address, would probably suit you. If, on the other hand, you're more of a hitter and like to hit down and through the ball with a strong lateral move to your left, then you'll probably prefer a lower tee, with less than half the ball above the top of the driver.

Be aware, however, that when you change drivers you may also have to change your tee height. Metal-headed clubs generally have a lower centre of gravity than wooden-headed models. With more weight towards the bottom of the club, they tend to get the ball up a bit more easily. As such, you should expect to tee the ball a little lower for the metal woods.

Mental Readiness

Proper mental preparation is also important on the teeshot, particularly when the hole offers a special challenge in terms of length or tightness. On holes that call for long carries, don't let yourself become the architect's pigeon. I confess that I still fall for this one. I'll look down the fairway, see the big bunker at the corner of the dogleg, and immediately ask my caddie how far I have to hit the ball to carry the sand. Instead, I should be contemplating the best way to work my ball *around* the trap. Don't go for the big carry unless it's comfortably within your power. Put the drive in play – then get aggressive on your approach shot.

When you're looking down the throat of a tight driving hole, you need to loosen up mentally. I find that the best way to do that is first to loosen up physically. If I'm not hitting first, I try to do this as my partners are hitting their drives. I close my eyes, take a deep breath, and then slowly roll my head to the side, first one way and then the other. I go through this exercise on the first tee of virtually every tournament I play. It relaxes my neck and shoulder muscles and gets me ready for a free, smooth swing.

Not too long ago, I learned another method of loosening up, from my good friend Seve Ballesteros. We were talking about the various mental techniques we use on the course, when Seve said, 'Whenever you see me at Augusta standing on a tee with my arms folded, I'm actually getting set for the next shot. What I do is take a deep breath and then press my hands hard against the bottom of my rib cage, for about fifteen seconds. When I let go and breathe out, there's a great feeling of release. That's when I step up to hit my drive.'

Even short holes demand some extra thought and concentration. Too many golfers make the mistake of teeing off every par-four and -five hole with their driver. But on a par-four of only 300 yards or so, that may not be the best ploy. Normally such short holes are well bunkered or close to water, and are best approached with a shot that will bite when it lands. If you knock your drive to within sixty yards or so of the green it's hard to hit the ball with sufficient force to impart the backspin that will make it stop. Therefore, it's wiser to tee off with a fairway wood or long iron, leave yourself a hundred yards or so from the green, and swing firmly on a sand wedge or pitching wedge that will fly over any greenside trouble yet stop quickly after it lands. This tactic may look cautious from the tee, but it's aggressive where it needs to be – on the shot to the flag.

Gamesmanship

One of the subtler aspects of aggressive driving involves the gamesmanship that goes on at the tee. When you're in a match, the teeshot is the opening gambit, and sets the stage for the rest of the battle on the hole.

Since I'm a long hitter, I like to have some fun with my opponents. Sometimes, on an extremely long hole, if I'm hitting second I'll take out an iron and lean on it as my opponent gets ready to play his shot. Occasionally I can actually see him thinking, 'This hole is 450 yards and Norman's teeing off with a 1-iron – my God, he must be even longer than I thought.' If I can get those types of thoughts going through my opponent's mind, he might do anything. Then when my turn comes, I put the iron back and take out my driver.

I do the opposite too. On a tight hole where I know everyone's debating about club selection, I'll quickly take out my driver and waggle it a bit for everyone to see. The other guys then may make the mistake of selecting too much club for the shot. After they hit, I'll put the driver, which I had no intention of hitting, back in the bag and select a more intelligent club.

I like to talk it up on the tee too, especially when I'm playing against a fellow who I know is something of a gamesman himself. I've stepped up to short par-fours and said loudly to my caddie, 'Can we get it to the green today?' He'll then say something like, 'No problem,' both of us knowing full well that we have no intention of trying such a shot. It's all an act for the benefit of the shorter-hitting opponent, just to get his brainwaves stirring as he prepares for his own teeshot.

But you don't have to be a power-hitter to be able to use gamesmanship. If you hit the ball straight, you can be just as effective. When you're the second to play on a tight hole, you can take out an iron. If your longer-hitting opponent sees you, he may back off his driver. Then, after he hits, you can put the iron back and hit it past him with your driver. You can also talk it up on the tee and put wayward thoughts in a slugger's mind. Try a line such as 'That O-B [out of bounds] on the right really sneaks up fast, doesn't it?' or 'Thickest rough on the golf course is on this hole.' Believe me, they work!

Of course the most common form of gamesmanship takes place on the tees of par-three holes. I'll never forget the time I used it on a fellow Open Champion. He and I were in contention in a major event in Australia when we got to a par-three hole. The shot was between an 8-iron and a 7-iron. I knew my opponent was debating his choice, and I also knew he had a tendency to be a bag-watcher. So, hitting first, I took a 7-iron and gave it a swing which was big and long but was actually quite soft and slow – all arms and no hand action. The ball landed on the front half of the green. He then chose a 7-iron, hit it way over the back of the green, and took four.

Such gamesmanship may seem to stretch the limits of etiquette, but the fact is, everyone does it. It's part of the game on Tour. And the top players know how to use it best of all. During the 1986 US Open, Lee Trevino got me good. At the 10th hole one day each of us had a tricky downhill birdie putt. Trevino hit first, and when his putt finished a foot or so past the hole he said to his caddie (for my benefit), 'Herman, that is the fastest putt I've seen all year long.' It worked – I left my approach putt five feet short and then missed the next one. Lee parred the hole and I bogeyed. But rest assured, I'll get old Supermex back!

The Right Club

The final aspect of good driving relates to the driver itself. Except for the putter, no club is more important than the driver. And just as with the putter, you should feel absolutely comfortable and confident when you take the driver in your hand. If you don't feel this way with the driver you now own, get another one.

And don't limit yourself to clubs with the number '1' on their soleplates. Frankly, I think most amateurs would hit the ball longer and straighter off the tee if they would drop the driver and go to a 2-wood. The 2-wood has more loft, gives you more elevation, less sidespin and longer carry than does the driver. And with today's heavily irrigated courses, that's an important factor.

The 2-wood is geared to hit the ball 240 yards on the fly and give you roll of about 10 yards whereas the driver will hit it about 220 yards on the fly and give you about 40 yards. On slow fairways, however, you won't get anywhere near that 40 yards of roll.

On the surface, recommending a 2-wood may not seem like advice for an aggressive golfer, but it is. After all, if this club will give you additional confidence, you'll be able to make a more aggressive swing on the tee, and that's what counts.

I can recall at least one instance where my decision to tee off with a fairway wood was instrumental to victory. In the final round of the 1986 Panasonic European Open at Sunningdale, I was in strong contention when I came to the 3rd hole, a short par-four. From tee to green the hole isn't much more than 275 yards, and that green is an inviting target.

I knew I could get there with my driver – my only question was whether I could hit it straight enough and *soft* enough to keep it from running through the green. Then I said to myself, 'If you take the 3-wood and hit it as high and hard as you can, with just a bit of draw, you might get to the green.'

Out came the 'spoon'. Knowing I couldn't possibly hit it over the green, I made an aggressive swing, stayed behind the shot a bit to ensure plenty of height, and absolutely nailed it. Not only did the ball reach the green, it came down two feet from the hole, and bit. In went the putt for an eagle two. That spurred me on to tie Ken Brown whom I beat with a birdie on the first playoff hole.

Whether you settle on a 1-wood or 2-wood, give some thought to the length of your driving club. I became a straighter, more solid driver the day I shortened the shaft of my club by three-quarters of an inch. If your driver is longer than forty-three inches, and you're currently erratic with it, consider having your pro cut it down an inch. My bet is that you'll be pleasantly surprised at the improved compactness and timing of your swing, and the better control your teeshots will have.

For the same reasons, I'm an advocate of getting the stiffest shaft of club you can handle. This is particularly true if you have a hooking problem. In fact, as fine a player as David Graham eliminated his hook when he went to an extra stiff driver. The stiffer shaft does not whip through and close the clubface as easily as a whippy shaft does, so in effect you can swing more aggressively. Of course, there's such a thing as too stiff a shaft. When you hit all your teeshots dead to the right, it usually means the shaft is too stiff for you to square up the club. In such a case, you should back off from that one level of stiffness. If that shaft is an X (for extra stiff) go down to an S (stiff); if it's an S, go to an R (regular).

The only golfers who should not seek the stiffest shaft possible are players in desperate need of distance, including some women and senior players. If this is the case with you – if you're not getting your longest teeshots much farther than 175 yards or so – try a more flexible shaft in your driver. With an R or L (ladies') shaft you'll have an easier time 'closing the door' of the clubface in the hitting area, and you'll be likely to develop a draw or hook which will give you a few extra yards of roll. Just be aware that these yards may come at the expense of accuracy.

You should also pay attention to what's called the face depth of the driver. The term should actually be 'face height' because that's what it is, the distance from the bottom of the face of the driver to the top. In any case, the shallower the depth of the face, the lower the centre of gravity of the club and the higher you'll hit the ball. The deeper (taller) the face, the higher the centre of gravity and the lower you'll hit the ball. Arnold Palmer, for instance, has a swing that produces low shots, so to counterbalance that tendency he uses a shallow-faced club. Bear in mind that all metal woods have very low centres of gravity, so for that reason they have little loft built into their clubfaces. When someone tells you he has a 9-degree-loft metal wood, you can assume it will hit the ball about the same height as a standard 12-degree wooden-headed driver.

I Dare You

Let Out the Shaft

There are teeshots, and there are *big* teeshots. This chapter has told you how to hit the former – now I'd like to give you a couple of tips on how to launch the latter. After all, nothing feels better – or does more for your confidence – than hitting the ball on the screws, watching it jump off your clubhead, soar forever and roll to a point beyond the balls of your playing partners, beyond your own previous career drive. I know when I pull out the stops and do everything just right, I can hit it over 350 yards – and believe me, that's one of the greatest kicks in the world.

Now, I'll also admit I don't try to hit this shot off every tee. It's foolish to swing all-out all the time because you sacrifice accuracy. (The only golfers who *should* go for maximum distance on every teeshot are youngsters just learning the game. For them, it's important to learn distance first, and let the techniques of accuracy come later.)

I save my biggest teeshots, ironically, for the shortest holes. On short par-fours, such as the

A swing thought I use all the time – RPB, for 'right pocket back'. Make your right trouser pocket turn as far back as possible, and you'll guarantee maximum hip turn for an extra-strong drive.

aforementioned 3rd at Sunningdale and 18th at St Andrews, a big blow will get me to the green and, as the little Scotsman said, 'Eliminate the second shot'. The same goes for the shortish fives where a good drive will enable me to get home in two and make my third shot a putt.

So lesson number one is pick your spots intelligently. Lesson number two is don't try too hard. In golf, trying fails – you just get in the way of yourself. Don't *try* to hit the ball 275 yards if you've never hit it 250. Don't *try* to hit it harder or longer than you ever have. *Do* try to hit it more *solidly* than ever.

As with the standard swing, you can pre-programme the key aspects of this swing as you take your address. First, tee the ball a bit higher than normal. For maximum distance, the ideal launch angle for any projectile is 45 degrees. But since the average driver has only 11 or 12 degrees of loft on it, you need to be sure of catching the ball just slightly on the upswing.

As you take your grip, remember the lesson Jack Nicklaus gave me – give some thought to your grip pressure. There's a misconception that when you want to hit the ball a long way you should firm up your hold on the club. Actually, just the opposite is true. You want to make a free-flowing swing, so don't strangle the club – that will only tighten up your armswing. Instead, caress it, hold it a bit less firmly than you would for a normal drive. (Incidentally, this is also a good idea when you're in a tense situation – the tighter the situation, the looser the grip.)

The next key is to widen your stance a bit, in order to set up a wider, more powerful arc. Do this by moving your right foot a bit to the right of its usual position – no more than an inch or two. As for the left foot, flare out the toe a bit more than usual. This will help you to uncoil powerfully into your downswing. The last pre-swing adjustment relates to ball position – move it forward to a point between your left instep and toe. This will have the same effect as the high tee, to help you approximate that 45-degree launch angle.

For a wider, more powerful arc, set up with a slightly wider stance by moving your right foot an inch or so to the right of its usual position for your driver swing.

The wider stance will lower your centre of gravity and will help you to make what is probably the most important move when it comes to long-distance driving – an extra-low, extra-long take-away. When I take the club back for a big drive, I try to glide back from the ball for as long as possible. It's important to feel as if you're stretching your arms out to their maximum as you make this crucial first move. Since the right foot is farther back than usual, this stretch won't be as taxing as it would be with a stance of normal width.

Unfortunately, that same wide stance – and the flared left toe – *will* make it more difficult for you to make a full backswing turn. The coil will not come naturally, so you have to work on it a bit. Since this is a conscious action, I've found it useful to have a key 'power swing thought' on long drives: when I step up to the ball, I say to myself, 'RPB, Greg.' RPB stands for 'right pocket back'. Through practice, I've found that when I can key on making my right-front trouser pocket turn around to the back as far as possible, I'll virtually ensure my maximum hip turn. And when the hips turn, the back and shoulders turn. Once that coil is maximised, the big gun is loaded. Actually the swing is exactly like a slingshot – the farther you can pull it back, the more forcefully it will snap through, and the longer your shot will go.

I hit upon this RPB key on the practice tee one day when I was trying to determine which type of move would best enable me to maximise my distance. Right pocket back works for me because I know that most of my power comes from my legs.

If your main power source is your legs, I suggest you give this a try. If, however, you get most of your distance from another source, it's important that you develop a key that better fits you. If, for instance, you have relatively 'quiet' leg action and have more of an upper-body swing, as does Arnold Palmer, you should develop a power key that makes you turn your back and shoulders. If hand action is your strength, as it is with David Graham, find a thought that will ensure a fast, powerful whip-through of the club in the hitting area. If you're extremely flexible and have an upright swing, as do young players such as Fred Couples and Davis Love, you might want to concentrate on getting your hands high for maximum height of your arc. Whatever your main power source is, develop a swing key that will help you maximise it. Then go hit your longest teeshots.

CHAPTER 4

Positive Approaches

SHOTS FROM THE FAIRWAY

If you're as naturally aggressive as I am, then one of the most challenging – and frustrating – aspects of this game is the approach shot. After all, when you're hitting the driver you can usually make a full-blooded swing and go for distance. And when you're around the green you can gun for the flag. But when you're standing in the fairway, it's a different story. With 100 or 200 yards to go and a necklace of bunkers staring you in the face, the operative word is not aggression – it's caution. You don't need awesome power or pin-splitting accuracy – you need control.

Caution and control. Nice words, but not my style. I think it's fair to say that whatever reputation I have as a player is based in large part on the strength of my driving game and on my putting, scrambling and play around the greens. Aggressiveness plays a positive role in all those areas.

However, as I said in the rankings of my game in Chapter 1, middle-iron play is one of my weaker suits. Still, as an aggressive golfer I view this not as a problem but as an opportunity. One of my main goals over the last couple of years has been to reconcile the requirements of the approach game with my naturally aggressive style of play. I've put a good deal of time and effort hitting and rehitting practice shots, thinking and rethinking strategies. I've learned a lot by watching the shot selection of players such as Jack Nicklaus and Lee Trevino, and I've learned even more just through my own trial and error during actual tournament play. As someone once said, good judgement comes from experience and experience comes from bad judgement.

The experience and knowledge I've gathered can be useful to any player. So let me share with you the basics as well as the subtleties of playing intelligently aggressive golf from fairway to green.

The Basics

Here's one of the most difficult questions in golf: 'Should your swing on a 5-iron be any different from your swing on a driver?' It's difficult because the answer is both yes and no. Yes, the swing for the 5-iron – in fact for each of the irons – is different from that for the driver. And no, *you* should not try to swing any differently.

When you stand to the ball with a shorter club in your hand, several aspects of your address position automatically change, and these pre-swing adaptations immediately alter the nature of your swing.

First, you have to bend over more, to lower your hands down to the shorter shaft. The shorter the club, the more you have to bend from the waist and counterbalance that tilt by sticking out your rump.

With the shorter clubs, you'll also be standing closer to the ball. It will be only a foot or so in front of your toes, as opposed to nearly three feet on the driver. This will result in your hands being closer to your body. See for yourself. Without even taking a club, pretend you're addressing first a driver, then a wedge, and notice how on the driver your arms extend out towards the ball much more than on the wedge, where they hang down near your thighs. Notice also that as you switch from one club to the other you subconsciously tilt from the waist more markedly for the wedge.

Along with these natural changes in address position, you should make one intentional change, which I mentioned in Chapter 2. As you address shorter and shorter irons, you should gradually decrease the width of your stance, bringing your right foot progressively closer to your left while keeping your ball position constant.

All of these address adaptations have the same effect. They set you up for the more vertical, U-shaped swing that shorter clubs require. On the fairway woods and long irons, the differences from the driver are minor. These clubs, after all, are nearly as long as the driver. The resulting swings are therefore similar to the big, wide sweep for a teeshot.

As the shaft shortens for the middle irons, however, both the nature of the shot and the nature of the set-up and swing change visibly. On these clubs, you don't want to maximise your distance, you want to control it just as surely as you want to control the direction in which the ball flies. The narrowed stance will help you do this, by reducing your leg action and encouraging more of an arm-and-shoulder swing. And even that armswing will be a bit less powerful because, with a shorter club, you'll have less centrifugal force at work.

As you move down to the short irons and wedges, where the stance should also open up a couple of degrees, your narrow, more crouched set-up will pre-programme a markedly more vertical swing that will produce a down-and-through impact that is in vivid contrast to the horizontal sweep of the driver.

Having made that point, let me say that you should never *intentionally* try to swing the club in a horizontal or vertical way. Never try to fit your swing to the club in your hand. After all, it's tough enough to master one golf swing without having to manipulate a dozen of them. Just remember to narrow your stance. The clubs themselves will cause you to do the rest.

Once I'm in the address position, I make no conscious swing changes whatsoever. In fact, I disagree strongly with teachers who suggest that you should use a shorter or less purposeful swing on the fairway woods and irons than on the driver. I take my club back to a position at or near parallel at the top of the swing, whether that club is a driver, a 3-wood, a 3-iron, a 7-iron or a wedge. And except when I'm trying to play some sort of specialty shot, I maintain the same swing tempo and rhythm for every club in the bag.

With a shorter club in your hand, you will automatically have less clubhead speed, so there's no need to throttle-down your swing. Besides that, swing-shortening is a very mechanical way to play golf and it tends to undermine your rhythm. The minute you start trying to calibrate your swing length, you introduce complexities, unnecessary, unnatural wrinkles in an already complicated movement. If, for instance, on a 5-iron shot you try to take six inches off the length of your backswing, your muscles sense this forced stopping of the club. At the top, you subconsciously doubt that you've stored the correct amount of power in your swing; as a result you may jerk the club down, you may decelerate, or who knows what. You undermine your rhythm and your overall confidence. I've been told that when my game is on, my swing has an automatic 'swish-click' look on every shot. If I had to attribute that to anything, I'd say it's the consistency of my swing length and rhythm from club to club.

With an absolutely consistent swing technique throughout your full shots on irons and woods, you

The shorter the club in your hand, the closer you'll stand to the ball and the more you'll bend over at address, and the nearer your hands will be to your body.

I take a full backswing, with the clubshaft going at least to a parallel position, on every club in the bag – it's part of keeping the game simple and consistent.

have the ability to control the distance of your shots completely according to your choice of club. And that gets us to the other key factor in approach play – club selection.

A decade of playing in pro–ams has convinced me that the number-one fault among amateurs is not in the set-up or swing – it's club selection. To put it bluntly, everyone underclubs. Nine out of ten golfers leave their approach shots short of the green, where most of the architect's fiercest perils lurk.

The reason, I think, goes back to what I said in Chapter 1 – we're all victims of our best shots. If, on one day you hit the 5-iron 185 yards, then you tend to think that 185 is your 5-iron distance. It's not. That's the distance of your best effort with a 5-iron. Your actual distance may be closer to 165. Heck, I've hit 5-irons 250 yards on occasion, but when I'm 250 yards from a green, I normally select a 3-wood.

The only way to get an accurate idea of your distance with each club is to take an hour or so of practice time and learn the truth. Get a pencil and a sheet of paper, list the clubs in your bag down one column, and take that sheet with you to a serious practice session.

If you want to do this right, go to a practice range or a large, flat, open area of any kind at a time when no one else is there, so you'll be able to hit shots and then pace them off. Before you go, determine the length of your average 'pace' by stepping off ten paces, measuring that distance, and then dividing it by ten. For most men, a normal pace is almost exactly a yard, but yours may be shorter or longer. If it is, I'd suggest that for the purpose of stepping off your shots, you alter your stride so that it approximates a yard.

Also, be sure to do this little experiment under controlled conditions. First, you'll need a dry, windless day. Secondly, you'll need to hit your shots from a surface that closely approximates the fairways from which you normally play your approaches. Hardpan or lush grass won't work. Thirdly, you'll want to be sure that your landing area is flat. Don't worry if it's a field of long grass – that's better than a hard-baked area – because what you want to measure is the carrying distance of your shots, not the carry-and-roll distance. If your practice shots hit and sit in the thick grass, that's perfect. Otherwise, you should deduct the roll yardage from whatever total distance the ball travels.

Once you've warmed up, start with the sand wedge, and hit at least a dozen balls with it. Two or three dozen would be better. Then pace them off. Disregard the ridiculously fat shots and skulled shots, but include all the others, and then make a note of the *average* distance those balls flew. Write that number next to the sand-wedge line on your sheet of paper – and imprint it on your mind. This, whether you like it or not, is your distance for the sand wedge.

Walk back to the tee and go through the same procedure for the pitching wedge, the 9-iron, the 8-iron, and all the rest of your clubs. This will take an hour or so, but believe me, it will be the best practice time you'll ever spend. At the end of it, you'll have some very valuable numbers. Memorise them.

I did this long ago, and I redo it from time to time, to monitor the effects of changes in my swing and golf equipment. Currently, these are my carrying distances with each of the clubs in my bag:

Club	*Yards*
Driver	260
3-wood	230
1-iron	220
2-iron	210
3-iron	220
4-iron	190
5-iron	180
6-iron	165
7-iron	155
8-iron	143
9-iron	135
Pitching wedge	125
Sand wedge	100

Again, these are carrying distances – the yardage the ball travels in the air – on an absolutely calm day, hitting from level, well-clipped fairway grass to a dead-flat landing area.

The Aggressor's Edge

Unfortunately, most approach shots are *not* played on absolutely calm days from level, well-clipped fairway grass to dead-flat landing areas. To follow the yardages on your sheet of paper blindly is almost as wrong as to underclub chronically. As we all know, virtually every situation calls for some sort of adaptation. And this is where club selection becomes an art as well as a science. This is where an aggressive player can distance himself (excuse the pun) from the pack.

Factors That Influence Club Selection

Wind is probably the largest influence on carrying distance. Figure on about one club for each ten miles per hour of wind. If you'd hit a 5-iron under normal conditions, use a 3-iron in a twenty m.p.h. headwind. A headwind also tends to accentuate any right-to-left or left-to-right action on your shot, so if you habitually play a fade or draw expect it to veer more than normal. In the case of the fade, in fact, it's wise to add another club; in the aforementioned twenty m.p.h. headwind, hit the 2-iron rather than the 5.

Of course, when you're playing with the wind at your back, you'll need less club. The same type of formula applies – one club for each ten miles of windspeed. In a twenty m.p.h. gust, that 5-iron becomes a 7. Expect lots of bounce and roll, too, because the ground will probably be drier than usual. As such, you may want to take even less club, and play for a bounce-on approach, if the entry to the green allows.

In the British Open, yardage is all but irrelevant because of the wind. I remember one day during the week of my victory at Turnberry playing the 15th hole with a driver – it's a 190-yard par-3. On another day, I reached the green with a 7-iron.

When the wind blows from the side, there's little effect unless you normally play a fade or draw. If you usually hit the ball from left to right, you may be able to use less club when playing with a left-to-right wind, but you may want one club longer when that fade is being buffeted by a right-to-left wind. The same will be true with a right-to-left shot – take less club when following a right-to-left wind, and possibly one more when fighting a left-to-right wind.

Grass conditions are also important. If your lie in the fairway is a bit shaggy, expect extra distance and use less club, particularly on the short and middle irons. (When blades of grass intervene between the clubface and ball, you can't put maximum backspin on the shot, so it will fly a bit farther than usual.) Conversely, from a tight, closely clipped fairway, you'll usually get a bit more backspin and a bit less distance. On the Tour we love these fairways because they enable us to make the ball dance. However, it is as well to use one more club than normal when the lie is tight.

Turf conditions are also important in the area of the green. When you're landing the ball on hard, dry ground, it will bounce high and roll forever, so plan your shot. You may want to take one or two clubs less than normal, land the ball several yards short of the green, and let it bounce on. Of course, when bunkers front the green, this strategy is complicated. On such occasions – particularly on par-fives with hard, shallow greens, I've intentionally hit my second shot into a bunker, in order to be sure of landing the next shot softly on the green.

When the landing area is wet, you'll want to be sure to take enough club to land your ball at or near the hole, allowing for no bounce and roll. Of course, if the whole golf course is wet, you may have that extra distance built into your lie. From moist fairways, you'll normally get that same flyer effect you get from fluffy fairways, as the water diminishes your ability to apply backspin. So club yourself down when playing out of dewy or moist lies. When the fairways are downright wet and

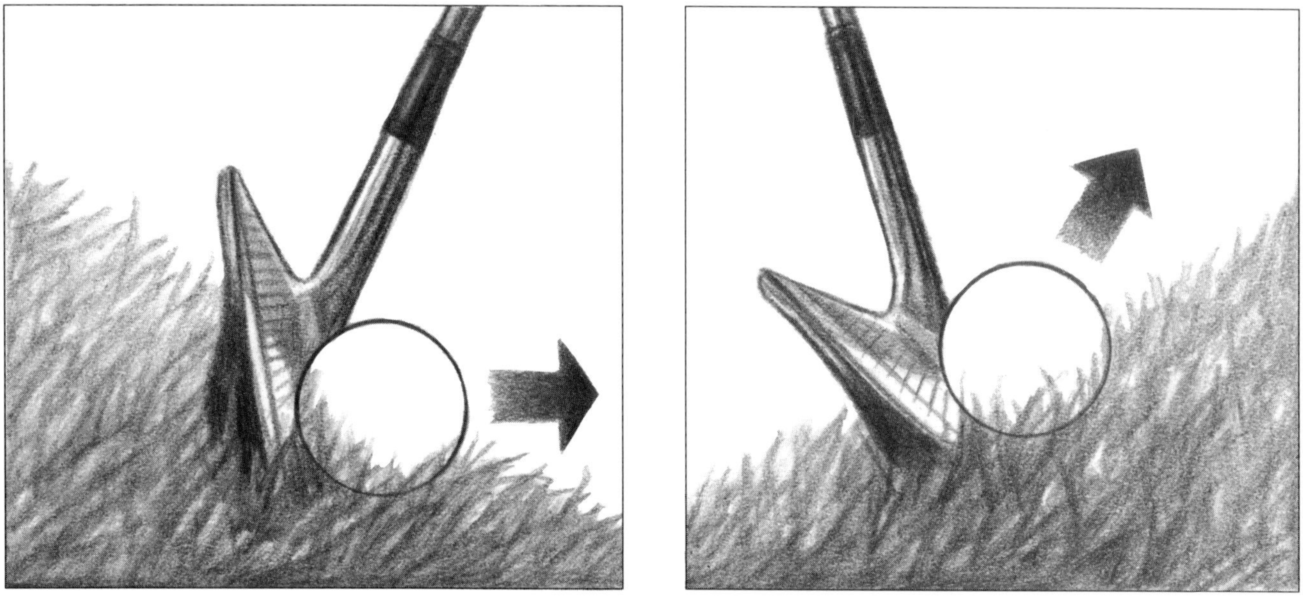

A downhill lie invariably produces low trajectory while an uphill lie contributes to loft.

sloshy, however, it's another story. Your footing and balance will be poor, your club will tend to knife into the turf, and you'll lose distance, so take the longer club and make a more controlled swing.

Now consider the influence of elevation changes. When you're playing to a green that is set high on a plateau, you'll need more club because the ball will come to earth before it has had a chance to complete the full extent of its flight and carry. The opposite is true when playing to a valley green. You'll have more 'hang time' in the air, so you'll be able to use a shorter club.

The challenge is compounded if you're also standing uphill or downhill. When you have an uphill stance, you'll tend to catch the ball more on the upswing and hit more of a lifting shot, which will give you extra height but less distance than from a flat lie. Take at least one more club, depending on the severity of the slope and whether or not you're also playing to an elevated green.

When you have a downhill lie, you'll tend to trap the ball and hit a lower shot than usual. It will therefore tend to roll more than normal, particularly if your landing area is also on a downward slope. Figure on at least one club less than usual – hit the 6-iron or maybe the 7-iron instead of the 5.

Temperature is also a factor. In extremely hot weather, you can expect to be looser, and your ball will be a bit livelier as well. Down-club yourself one club on average. In the cold, you'll be stiff, the ball will be hard, and you'll have no feel. Swing smoothly on at least one club more than usual, maybe two.

When you're between clubs, it's usually smartest to take the longer club. As I said, the architect traditionally places his most difficult hazards in front of the green where everyone can see them and be intimidated by them, so if you're in between clubs on a well-guarded hole, certainly go with the longer stick. However, my overall feeling on this matter is that you should go with your initial choice, no matter which club that may be. Your

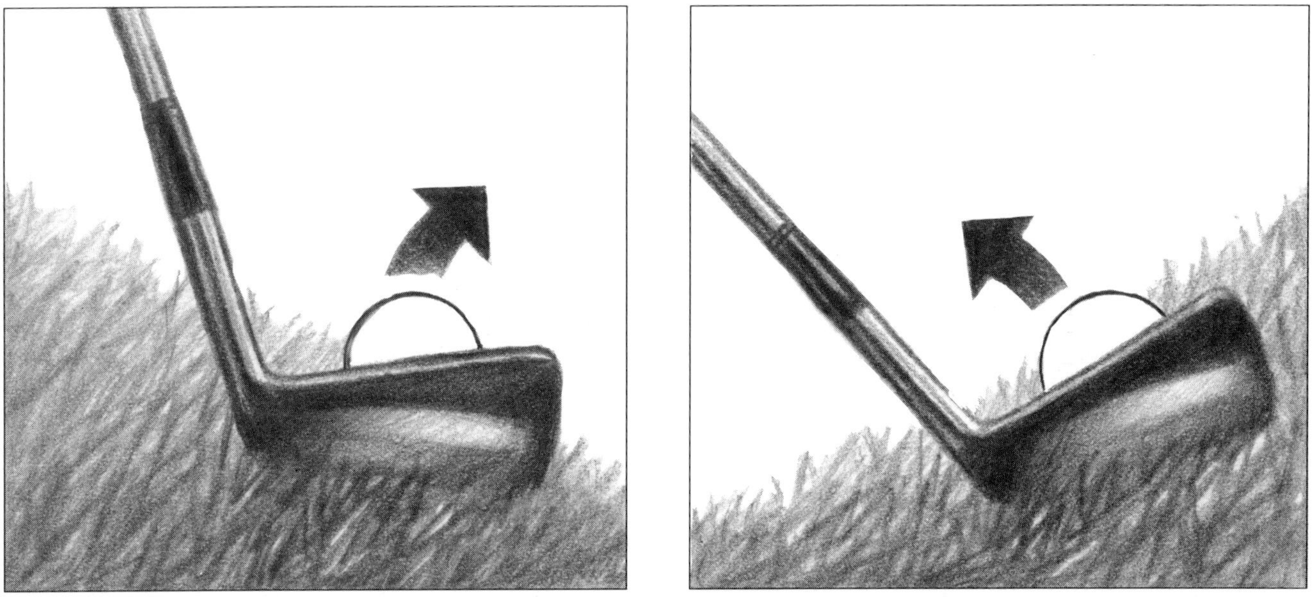

When the ball is below the feet, the shot tends to fly to the right. Above the feet, it flies left.

first choice is the intuitive, confident one and will therefore promote the more natural, free-flowing swing.

To a degree, it's also a question of individual makeup. If you're naturally a hard-swinging player, I think it's best to take the shorter club and go at it rather than trying to manufacture a short shot. If on the other hand you're a smooth swinger, you should definitely put that smooth swing on the longer club. If, under pressure, you tend to get your adrenaline pumping, go with the shorter club; if you tend to tighten up, go with the longer club.

This between-clubs situation often occurs on the tee of a par-three, and there you have a couple of things you can do about it. First, remember that you can take advantage of the full teeing area. Take the longer club if you want, and step back two driver lengths. As a practical matter, this won't make much of a difference, but it may give you the confidence to make a full swing on the longer club.

Another way of shortening the longer club is to tee the ball high, to produce a softer, floating type of shot. You can get similar results by teeing it at the edge of a divot to promote a clean, upward hit and a floating shot that will not fly as far. Conversely, you can lengthen the distance of the shorter iron by hitting it directly out of the grass, without a tee, particularly if you can find a fluffy area of the tee that will promote a flyer effect. I've often used this ploy when playing into a headwind, because it promotes a spinless shot that is less susceptible to the effects of the breeze.

Most of all, however, try to get yourself out of that huge majority of golfers who consistently leave their approach shots short of the green. I admit there's a certain macho kick in putting a hard swing on a short club and muscling the ball to the green. That's human nature, but it isn't the nature of golf. My experience is that golfers who like to brag about their 150-yard 9-irons rarely produce scores worthy of boast. Physical aggressiveness is of minimal use in golf.

Planning Your Attack

Mental aggressiveness, however, is vital. The key is to attack the golf course, not the ball. So when you select your club, go not simply for the flag but for the *top* of the flag. This, together with a realistic knowledge of your distance capabilities, will ensure that you'll rarely underclub. And if you get the ball to the hole every time, you'll be miles ahead of 99 per cent of your fellow golfers.

If you play most of your golf on the same course, one of the best favours you can do yourself is to make note of the course's idiosyncrasies regarding the approach game.

Take note of the holes that require you to fly the ball to the hole and those that allow you to run or bounce on. Many old-style courses gave players an option of the high-road and low-road approaches, whereas most modern courses feature more tightly guarded greens and generally allow only a lofted approach. Obviously, if you have a choice, your club selection is much wider. So be aware of the holes that allow you this latitude, and be ready to make use of it.

Also take note of the depth of the greens. On each hole, how much leeway do you have? Generally speaking, the shortest holes have what I call a one-club green, meaning you had better approach it with the one club that gives you the correct distance. One club less and you'll be in the front bunker; one club more and you'll bounce off the back. Most holes allow you at least two clubs or three.

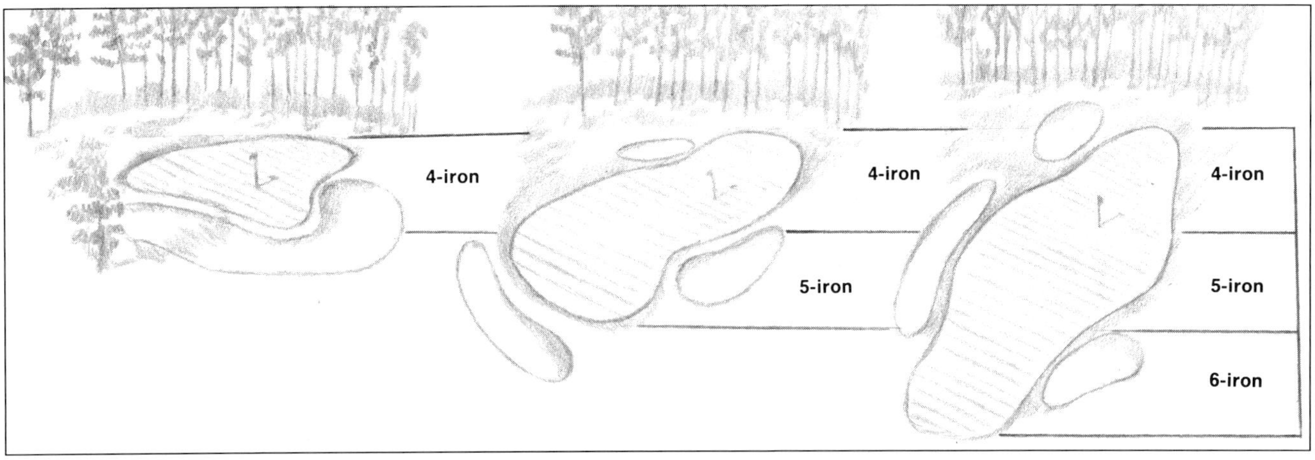

◀*Left:*
Teeing the ball at the front edge of a divot will encourage a high, floating shot.

Make note of the one-club, two-club and three-club greens on your course, and know your club selections for the various pin positions.

And on some courses, such as the Old Course at St Andrews, the enormous double greens are so deep you can hit them with up to five different clubs. (Of course, three or four of those clubs will leave you with a mammoth putt.)

So be aware of the holes on your course that have one-club, two-club and three-club greens, and jot down the clubs you'd normally play into those greens. Then pay close attention to pin positions. When the pin is in the back of a one-club green, club selection is not affected much, but when it's at the back of a three-clubber, you had better give your choice some extra thought.

Chances are, each green on your course has a minimum of three or four positions and at least one of those is a killer. Occasionally, I'll be preparing to play a shot, and either my caddie, Pete, or I will take a look at the green and say, 'That's a sucker pin.'

Sucker pins coax the golfer into an overly bold approach with little margin for error. When the flag is cut extremely close to a bunker or water or heavy rough, when it's in a spur of the green or on the ledge of a two-tiered green, it's a sucker position. If you usually fade the ball, a sucker pin is anything on the left side of the green. If you hit a draw, the sucker pin's on the right. It may look inviting from the fairway, but you're a sucker if you try to shoot at it, because if you miss the shot, even a little, you'll put yourself in trouble. The risks far outweigh the rewards.

Make note of the sucker pins on your course, and when you come to one, play smart and give it a wide berth. Don't fool with it, even if that means laying up. The 11th hole at the Augusta National Golf Club has a fast green with a pond hard by its left side. Years ago, when Ben Hogan came to that hole and the pin was on the left, he would purposely *miss* the green with his approach, taking his chances on a one-putt par. 'If you see me on that green with my second shot, you'll know I missed the shot,' he said. Here he was, the most accurate shotmaker of his time, perhaps of *all* time, and Hogan opted not to fool with a treacherous pin.

There are a couple of other holes I can think of where, if I don't hit a good drive, I may not want to go for the green. One is the 17th hole at St Andrews and another is the 18th at Bay Hill in Florida. On each of them, if the second shot misses the green it can be the beginning of a big score. And believe it or not, I've actually layed up on a par-3. During a recent AT&T Pebble Beach Pro–Am, when I got to the 16th hole at Cypress Point the wind was blowing a gale. Since that hole plays 233 yards over water, I didn't even think of trying for the green. I took a 3-iron and baled out to the left, then wedged on and took my bogey four.

But don't let me leave you with the impression that all holes must be played cautiously. There are easy placements too. On the Tour, we usually see them during pro–am days. You'll see them in big golf outings, when the object is for everyone to have a good time, and for play to proceed as quickly as possible.

What's an easy placement? Anything in the centre or 'fat part' of the green, away from trouble; a pin on the bottom tier of a two-tiered green; a pin in a swale or punch bowl. These placements allow for different ways to get to the hole. You can hit past the pin and suck back, hit short and bounce up, maybe even miss to the left or right and drift towards the hole. Most importantly, there's no threat of disaster if you miss the pin by a little bit.

When you look at these positions, and you have a good lie in the fairway, go ahead and gun for the flag. You should also attack when the pin position fits the type of shot you play most often. If you're a fader and the flag is positioned on the right side of the green, go for it, letting your shot drift across the green and towards the hole. Players who draw the ball should gun for the pin when it's cut on the back-left of the green.

By now you should realise that playing good approach shots involves a lot more than a controlled swing and a knowledge of your carrying distances with the various clubs. More often than not, it's a multifaceted calculation. Let me give you one example.

It was the final hole of the 1986 Western Australian Open. I had a one-stroke lead on Terry Gale who was playing behind me, and I knew I'd need at least a par to win. But I pushed my drive under a tree and had to chip out. That left me 158 yards to the flag, and plenty of things to consider:

- My lie was downhill – that decreased the distance
- I had a twenty-five m.p.h. headwind – that increased the distance
- I had a flyer lie – that decreased the distance
- I was pumped up – that also decreased the distance
- Some large gum trees stood behind the green – I certainly didn't want to be long
- The green sloped severely from back to front and it was extremely fast – I certainly didn't want to be even a little long and leave a downhill putt
- The pin was at the back – I didn't want to be short either

Now, I first figured that if I could punch the ball low, it would stay below the tops of the gum trees and the wind wouldn't blow it back. But then it might shoot all the way across the green and off the back where I'd be dead. And if I hit the right club for the lie and distance – a 7-iron – I knew the ball would get up too high and would finish somewhere on the front of the green. That would give me an uphill putt but a long one, and I couldn't afford that. I had to get the ball to the hole.

What I decided to hit was a 6-iron, knowing it was in a sense too much club. But I told myself to go ahead and knock it up into the wind, put it up above the gum trees, and hope to hell that it would float back to a point approximating 158 yards.

It came off precisely as I had planned and finished only eight feet from the hole. I turned to my caddie and said, 'That's the best shot we've hit all week. There's no way I'm going to miss that putt.' And bang, in it went. After Gale parred the hole, I had a one-stroke victory. It was the last of my ten wins in 1986.

The nicest thing about that shot is that I can remember it so vividly. And the nicest thing about that is that I'll use that memory time and again when faced with similar situations. It's absolutely vital, before you decide on the shot you want to

Part of knowing how to play this shot is knowing when. *Don't try it unless you have a good lie where at least some part of the ball is sitting above the top of your driver.*

play, to run a vivid mental picture of it. If the picture fits your situation, you know you're ready to go. What I like to do is visualise a great shot from my past. In this way, I not only see the ball flight I want but I recall that ball flight in a positive context. This gives me the confidence to make the swing that will bring that vision back to life.

For middle-iron approach shots I often recall the shot I hit in the 1981 Masters. It was the final round and I was playing with Jack Nicklaus. At the 16th hole, the picturesque par-three over water, Jack hit first and put his ball four feet from the pin. As you can imagine, the gallery went absolutely crazy, which did little for my own concentration. But I somehow steeled myself and hit one of the finest shots of my life. The ball landed near Jack's ball and then almost went in the hole, finishing less than a foot away.

It felt great – and it *feels* great each time I think of that shot. So I use this positive mental movie every time I face a similar shot, particularly when the pressure is on.

So know your distances, consider all the factors, and then call upon past successes in visualising the shot you want to make. These are the keys to playing your approach shots with confident control.

I Dare You

Hit Your Driver Off the Deck

I call the driver from the fairway my 15th club. It's unbelievable how useful it can be in helping you to stay under the wind, maximise roll on fast fairways and reach seemingly unreachable holes. One place where I often hit it is on the 6th hole at the Bay Hill Club, site of the Hertz Bay Hill Classic. A long par-five that winds around the huge lake and usually plays into the teeth of the wind, the 6th is all but unreachable unless I can smash two drivers, back to back. But it's a fairly open fairway, so I'll invariably take out the driver for the second shot. I'll even aim it across the edge of the lake if I have to, knowing that, if I don't catch the ball perfectly, it'll skip across. That's the beauty of this shot. As long as you don't hit it fat, you'll always get plenty of distance.

I must play the driver 'off the deck' twenty-five

Widen your stance a bit, and shade your weight slightly to your right side.

Prior to impact you should feel as if your body is hanging back as your legs flash through the ball.

or thirty times a year. I'll never forget the time I used it in the 1985 Australian Open. Going into the final round I was in a four-way tie for the lead, and at the 14th hole it was still anyone's game.

After hitting a driver up the middle of the fairway of this long par-five playing dead into the wind I hit the driver again. It stayed under the wind but surged just high enough to clear the nest of bunkers at the green before settling twenty feet from the pin. In went the putt for an eagle. I followed with another birdie on the next hole and went on to win the tournament by two strokes.

The shot isn't as tough as it seems. A lot of the technique is simply mind over matter. You have to act as if you're hitting the ball off a tee. For that matter, your lie should be good enough so that the ball is in a sense teed up. Don't ever try to play this shot from a tight fairway lie. The ideal in fact is a perched lie in light rough. At least part of the ball should be above the top of your clubface. Control is important, so grip down about a half-inch on your club. This will also ensure that you won't hit the dreaded fat shot. On the other hand, you don't want to top the ball completely either, so be sure there's a bit of extra bend in your knees.

More than on any other shot, you want to make a sweeping swing. So widen your stance just a bit, and instead of dividing your weight equally between your feet, shade it about 60–40 to your right side. Your ball position, square stance and all other aspects of your address should be exactly the same as if you were hitting a teeshot.

In the takeaway, make an extra effort to sweep the club back low along the ground. The lower and longer you can take the club straight back and away from the ball, the greater chance you'll have of returning the clubface smack on to the back of the ball at impact.

Trust your lie, trust the loft on your driver and trust your swing. Remember that since you have a powerful weapon in your hands, you don't have to swing hard. In fact, on the downswing you should feel as if your upper body hangs back a bit as your legs drive through the ball. By staying behind this shot you'll help ensure a sweeping hit.

One final hint on this shot – it's easiest to hit with a driver that is relatively shallow-faced (not very tall from the bottom to the top of the face). Most metal woods are good from the fairway, but don't try to play this shot with a deep-faced driver unless your game is at the 5-handicap level. No matter what club you wield, however, give this teeless teeshot some practice. Once you can hit it with confidence, you'll love what it does for your game, especially when you put it to work against your opponents in match play.

CHAPTER 5

Making the Ball Work For You

SHOTMAKING TECHNIQUES

It was always my ambition to win my first major championship by a wide margin, so I'd be able to savour the final moments of triumph. In the 1986 British Open I got my wish. My five-stroke victory allowed me to enjoy the 17th and 18th holes at Turnberry, secure in the knowledge that no one could catch me.

Hole number 16, however, was another story. On the tee of that 415-yard par-four known as Wee Burn, I let my drive get away from me. Off it sailed into the darkest reaches of the right-hand rough.

Granted, I was five strokes clear of my closest pursuer, but 16 is no place to spray a teeshot, regardless of how big your lead may be. The approach must be played to a green that is tightly guarded by the only water hazard on the course, a small stream after which the hole is named. Hit the ball short or left, and you're in the drink, facing the loss of at least one stroke and probably more. Hit it long, and you'll probably catch the back bunker, leaving a downwind, downhill explosion with the burn staring you in the face. It's a challenging shot, even from a good lie in the middle of the fairway, something I most certainly did not leave myself in that final round.

They say, however, that major championships are won with a combination of talent, tenacity and luck. If that's true, then without question my share of good fortune occurred at 16 on Sunday. As Pete and I tramped across the hay and gorse en route to my wayward drive, I had no idea what to expect. But when we shouldered through the last circle of spectators, I beheld one of the prettiest sights imaginable. There was my ball, sitting smack in the centre of a gallery path. Amid some of the most daunting terrain in linksland golf, I had somehow found a gorgeous lie. A hundred and fifty thousand people had been trampling that area for a week, so instead of being buried in tangly grass, my ball was sitting cleanly on hard, bare ground. I couldn't have dropped it in a better place.

I looked at Pete and my first three words were, 'Perfect, perfect, perfect.' My next words came almost immediately. 'I've got the shot,' I told him.

The wind was coming at us from about a two-o'clock angle and with the clean lie I had, I knew I could put plenty of spin on the ball. My plan was to hit a big, high fade and send it at the centre of the green, knowing that its left-to-right movement would be more or less cancelled out by the right-to-left wind.

The shot came off just as I had hoped. My ball hung up in the sky, fighting against the wind but not drifting either right or left a bit. Down it came, ten feet from the hole. It was precisely at that moment that I knew I had won the championship.

Good luck gave me an opportunity. But good shotmaking enabled me to make the most of it. The ability to play fades, draws, punches and lofting shots is what separates mere golfers from true players. Combine this ability with an aggressive overall game, and you can lift your talent to the peak of its potential.

The Basics

Shotmaking is fundamentally the process of spinning the golf ball in special ways. Thus if you can understand the way in which this spin influences the flight of the ball, you'll have a headstart at learning how to impart that spin.

When you hit a straight shot with normal trajectory, you impart pure backspin. As you make impact with a 7-iron, for instance, the clubface pinches against the back of the ball and makes the ball rotate 'backwards', towards the club. The ball actually climbs up the face of the club for a millisecond. Then this backspin lifts the ball into the air. As the ball leaves your clubface it is spinning backwards at the rate of nearly 150 revolutions per second.

Every shot in golf has backspin – the drive, the chip, the sand shot, even the duck hook and the shank. In fact, even a putt skids backwards for an inch or so before it begins rolling forward.

When you cut across the ball, however, either from out to in or in to out, you impart sidespin along with the backspin. It is this sidespin that causes the ball to curve to the right or left.

Clockwise sidespin makes the ball move from left to right. In basic terms, you impart this spin whenever the face of the golf club is open in relation to the angle of your swing path at impact. Please recall that open, in the case of the clubface, means 'pointing to the right of' the swing path. This should not be confused with an open stance in which your body is aligned to the *left* of the target line.

It's important also to understand that this open clubface is the *only* root cause of fades and slices. The fact is, you can make a perfectly square, on-plane swing but if at impact the face of your club is pointing to the right of your target line, you'll curve the ball from left to right. Conversely, you can have your club pointed perfectly down the target line, but if you hit the ball with a glancing blow from out to in, that straightforward clubface will actually be open in relation to (pointing to the right of) the path of your swing. This also will produce a slice. The more open your clubface is in relation to your swing path, the more clockwise sidespin you'll put on the ball. Slightly open faces produce fades, wide-open faces produce slices.

Draws and hooks comes from the opposite situation, where the clubface is closed in relation to (pointed to the left of) the path of the swing at impact. This imparts counterclockwise spin which makes the ball turn from right to left. As with the slice spin, it doesn't matter whether your swing path is from out to in, in to out, or straight into the back of the ball; if your clubface is pointed further left than the line on which that club is moving, you're going to curve the ball from right to left. A little spin produces a draw, a lot of spin means a hook.

Instructional advice abounds when it comes to playing fades and draws. Many teachers advocate a stronger grip, with the hands rotated to the right on the club. Others recommend finagling with your weight distribution or swing speed. Still others recommend stiff-armed swings for a slice, wristier methods for a hook.

I avoid these methods completely. For one thing, they're complicated. As I've said several times in this book, golf should be kept as simple as possible. For a second thing, it's folly to believe you can regulate the curve of a golf ball by regulating your wrist cock or weight shift. Finally, I distrust such methods because they fail to relate to the root causes of sidespin which I've just discussed.

To my mind, there's only one good way to play intentional fades and draws, and that's by presetting them with your alignment at address. The alterations I make are minor, and once I set them, I'm through. My grip and swing remain the same,

A draw or hook occurs when you apply counterclockwise spin, hitting the ball with a clubface that is closed to (pointing to the left of) the path on which it is travelling.

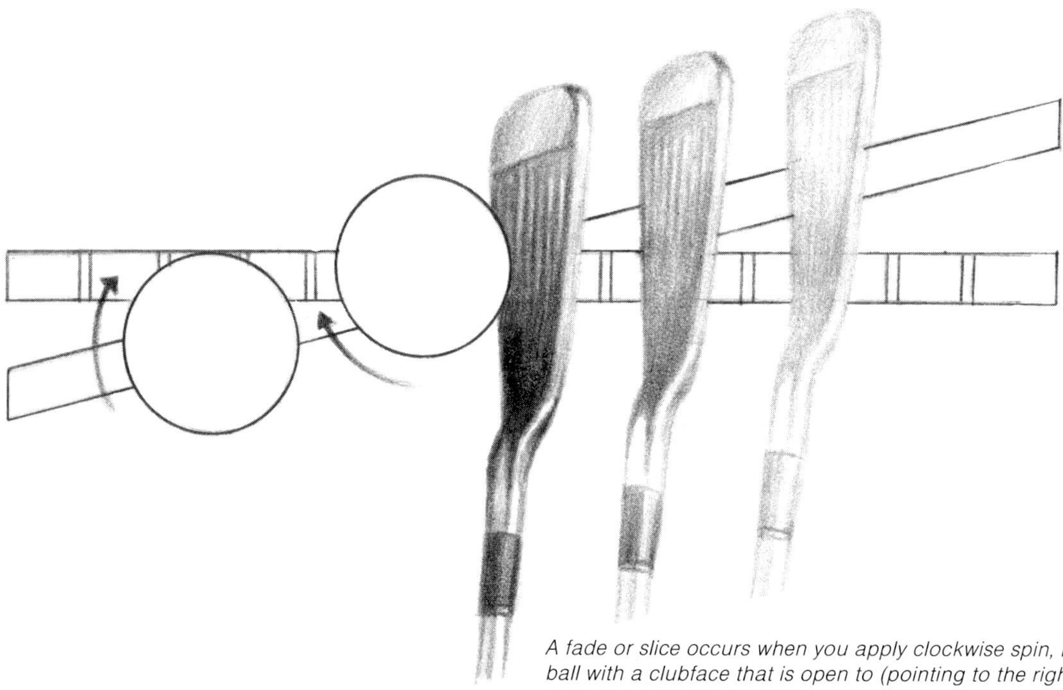

A fade or slice occurs when you apply clockwise spin, hitting the ball with a clubface that is open to (pointing to the right of) the path on which it is travelling.

without any manipulation or conscious change of any kind.

For a left-to-right shot, I begin my address as usual, by setting my club behind the ball and aiming the clubface straight down the target line. Then I make a change. Instead of aligning my body parallel to the direction in which I've aimed the clubface, I set up in an open stance, with my feet, knees, hips and shoulders aligned several degrees to the left of the target line.

This set-up will cause me to take the club back on a line that is outside that of a straight-back takeaway. That will result in a swing that returns the club to the ball along that same outside path. At impact, the clubface will be aimed straight down the target line but will be swinging across that target line, thus imparting clockwise spin. The ball will start out to the left of the target (the line on which the swing directed it) and then, as the spin takes over, it will drift back towards the target (the

The fade: the open stance encourages a takeaway to the outside and a cut across the ball at impact.

point at which the clubface was aimed).

It's as simple as that. The more drift I want, the more open I stand while keeping the clubface aimed straight down the target line.

For the draw, it's naturally just the opposite. I set the clubface straight at the ball, then align my body several degrees to the right. This promotes a takeaway that will be more to the inside than usual, resulting in an impact that is from inside-to-out and imparts counterclockwise spin. The ball starts out to the right, then draws back in towards the target at which I aimed my clubface. The more curve I want, the more I aim myself to the right.

It's that easy. Just set up correctly and then trust your swing. In fact, if there's one key to the swing, it's a mental one. Forget about where you want the ball to finish, and concentrate instead on where you want to direct the shot. Go back to the idea of visualising the apex of your shot, and in this case think of hitting the ball to the farthest sideward point of the fade or draw. If you set up properly and direct your ball to that crest of the arc, it will turn

The draw: the closed stance sets up an inward takeaway and an in-to-out impact.

on its path from that point to the target.

When you need to keep the ball down, under a tree limb or into a headwind, it pays to know how to hit a low shot. Let's say you're 150 yards from the green and you need to keep it low. You'd like to hit it about the length of a 6-iron with the trajectory of a driver. But since the 6-iron has about 25 degrees more loft than the driver, you need to make some adjustments.

As with the bending shots, most of the adjustments are done at address. The first thing I do is widen my stance by about an inch. This lowers my centre of gravity and sets me up for a flatter swing with a more driving type of impact. Since this lowering brings my hands closer to the ball, I grip down a half-inch or so on the club. This adjustment will also help me to keep my swing under control. And since I want as little loft as possible, I position the ball several inches behind its normal place in my stance. This will keep my hands and body out in front of the ball on the downswing and will in effect take some of the loft off the club. My final change is in my alignment. When I flatten my swing, I have a tendency to draw the ball to the left, so I compensate by aiming both the clubface and my body a couple of degrees to the right.

Since you want a horizontal attack on the ball, it's important to take the club back that way – low and long. This is the only swing where I don't take the club back to parallel. When I'm hitting a low shot, my hands don't go much farther than shoulder height. On the downswing, I drive through hard with the hands, keeping the club low through the extension, and the ball will stay low as well.

One of the keys on the low shot is staying in front of the ball at impact. It follows therefore that when you want to hit a high shot, you should make adjustments that will allow you to stay *behind* the ball. The first thing I do is position the ball about a half-inch forward of its usual spot in my stance. I then widen my stance a half-inch. Together these changes put my centre of gravity about an inch to the right of where it is for a normal shot. I'm an inch more behind the ball. This also gives me the feeling that I'm down and under the ball, and that I'll be catching it on the upswing.

Some people prefer to play the high shot from an open stance, to encourage a descending blow that will add backspin. To my mind, that's an unnecessary complication. The way I see it, if you want a little more loft, take a 7-iron instead of a 6. But don't add complications to your swing.

The swing is a normal, full movement. Don't try to lift the ball up, just trust your set-up and the loft on your club. At impact you should feel as if your body is hanging back as your arms whip upwards into a high finish.

The Aggressor's Edge

You don't have to be a 70s shooter to add these shots to your repertoire. All golfers should know how to play the low and high shots, and any player who can hit the ball 180 yards or so is capable of developing the fade and draw. Indeed, if you're a shorter hitter, the draw should be the first shot you learn.

Hybrid Shots

And once you've mastered the methods of hitting the four basic types of shots, it's a relatively simple matter to hit more difficult shots, just by mixing the address adjustments you've learned. Let's say, for instance, that you want to hit the same shot I did back at that 16th at Turnberry – a high fade. All you have to do is combine the methods of hitting a fade and hitting a high shot.

Position the ball a bit forward of its normal point in your stance (for extra height), then aim your clubface straight down the target line while aligning your body a few degrees to the left (for a left-to-right arc). Once you've made these adjustments, swing as you always do.

For a high draw, simply play the ball forward and aim your body to the right. You set up for a low fade by playing the ball back in your stance and aiming left; for a low draw, play the ball back and aim right.

As I said, I don't like fiddling with my swing for the purpose of shotmaking. However, if you've already learned the basic methods and how to use them, I will share a couple of extra tricks I occasionally use. They aren't swing changes, just things I like to think about during certain types of shots.

The first trick relates to the grip. Although I don't believe in changing the position of the hands in any way for any shot, I do like to alter my grip pressure a bit. When I want to hit a fade, and the conditions are not ideal for that type of shot, I'll give myself some insurance by taking an extra firm hold on the club in my left hand. This will inhibit any tendency for my right hand to overpower my left during the downswing, causing a closing of the clubface and a draw or hook.

I'll also grip more firmly – in both hands – when

The low shot: with the ball well back in the stance, make a controlled three-quarter swing and a low finish with your hands driving through the ball and out to the target.

I want to jam a really low shot. Again for this shot, you don't want any extra play in the hands and wrists, particularly any sort of upward scooping motion. A firm grip guards against that.

For the opposite reason, I'll generally loosen my grip pressure a hair when hitting the ball high. This promotes a slightly wristier swing, allowing the wrists to flick the club under the ball. The result is a fast-climbing shot.

I'll also grip more loosely if I have to hit a big hook. The lighter pressure will allow my right hand to work the clubface like a closing door, with the toe of the club passing the heel as I make impact. This will add to the counterclockwise spin on the shot, and therefore will increase the amount of right-to-left bend.

The other trick I use relates to my leg action, specifically to my knees. When I want extra insurance for hitting a low shot, I'll be sure to brace my left knee on the downswing. Hard-driving, horizontal swings need to have something to hit against, so the left knee should not collapse or twist out of the way.

When I want to hit a very high shot, I'll key on the right knee at address, flexing it a bit more than usual and kinking it in towards the ball. This will put me in more of a down-and-under position at both address and impact, which will encourage the slightly upward impact.

Picking Your Spots

Thus far I've told you only *how* to play these shots. But it's equally important to know where – and where not – to play them. For instance, under some conditions, a fade is impossible to play; under others a fade is the *only* shot to play. This is true for the draw and high and low shots as well. Knowing how to recognise these conditions is a skill that every aggressive golfer must develop.

I like to think of these influences as red lights, amber lights and green lights, since they tell you just how aggressive or cautious you should be. A red light says, don't try the shot, an amber light tells you to be careful, and a green light says go for it. Let's take a look at the fade, draw, low shot and high shot, and at the conditions that favour and discourage each.

For a fade, the best type of lie is a bare one such as I had on that 16th hole at Turnberry. This allows you to put the whole clubface on the ball and impart maximum spin. A short-trimmed bermuda-grass fairway is also good for a fade as is a clean lie in a fairway bunker. Shaggy lies, including almost any lie in the rough, are no good for fading or slicing, since the blades of grass intervene between your clubface and the ball and inhibit your ability to apply spin. A similar phenomenon occurs when you play in wet conditions, as water gets between the club and ball and lessens the friction. For this reason, it's much easier to manoeuvre the ball from a dry fairway than from a wet or dew-coated one.

A downhill lie will encourage a fade, since you'll tend to shift your weight down that hill on the downswing. When that happens, your body will get out in front and the clubface will tend to be open at impact. The best lie is a sidehill lie with the ball below your feet, since that promotes a more upright swing than normal. From this lie, you'll almost always fade, so there's no need to open your stance. Conversely, the red lights as far as hilly lies are concerned are a lie with the ball above your feet and an uphill lie.

Certain types of winds are also helpful. If you want to play a straight shot as I did at Turnberry, fade the ball against a right-to-left wind. A left-to-right wind will obviously amplify your fade, so unless you have plenty of room to work with, don't try to ride this wind. A tailwind will tend to straighten out the shot, and a headwind will exaggerate any bend you put on the ball.

Finally, keep in mind that some clubs are easier to fade and slice than others. Generally speaking, the straighter-faced irons and woods are easiest because they have less loft. The less backspin you put on the ball, the more powerful your sidespin will be. It's easy to fade – or slice – a driver or 2-iron, but much tougher to slice a 7-wood or a 9-iron. If you habitually slice your long shots but pull your short irons dead left, this is the reason.

Most of all, keep in mind that a fade or slice will fly a shorter distance and come down more steeply than a straight shot hit with the same club. Therefore, when playing an intentional fade, you should take at least one club longer than normal. On an intentional slice, take at least two clubs longer.

A draw or hook is also hard to hit with the short irons. However, it's relatively easy to move the

A bare lie encourages a fade or slice, whereas a draw is more easily hit when the ball is sitting up.

6-, 5- and 4-irons from right to left, and although the long irons and woods are easier to fade than draw, they certainly may be played both ways.

You can draw the ball from any good fairway lie, but a ball that's sitting up on the grass will be a help rather than a hindrance. At impact, the swing path for a draw/hook is more an across-and-outward move, and when the ball is slightly perched, it's

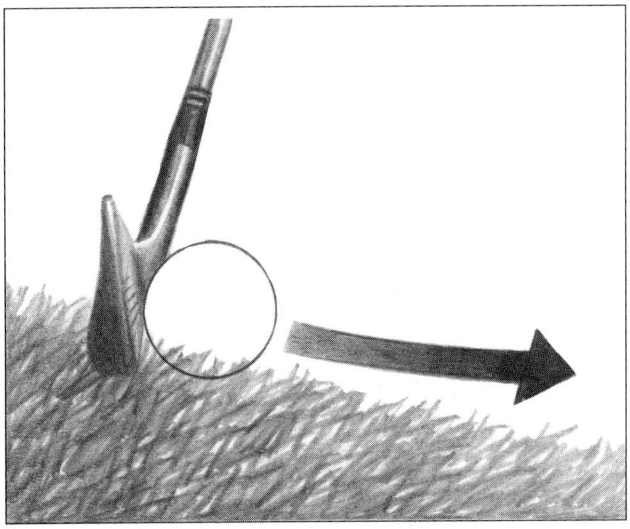

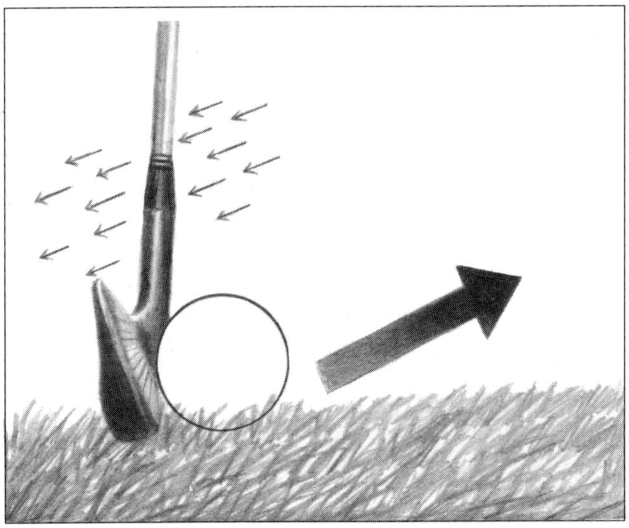

Downhill lies encourage a low trajectory, and a strong headwind tends to push shots high into the air.

easier to make this happen. For the same reason, it's not always easy to go right to left from hardpan, fairway bunkers or any sort of tight lie.

You'll put extra curve on any hook or draw hit with a right-to-left wind, and you'll get basically a straight ball into a left-to-right wind. As with the fade/slice, be aware that a tailwind will straighten your shot and a headwind will increase its bend.

Don't try anything fancy from the rough or wet grass unless you're also in one of the hilly lies that favours a draw. These are the sidehill lie with the ball above your feet and the uphill lie.

Finally, remember that right-to-left shots tend to be 'hot'. They bounce and roll much more actively than straight shots. So allow for this by taking at least one club less when playing a draw, at least two clubs less on an intentional hook.

The red and green lights on the low shot are obvious. Stay with the low-lofted clubs such as the 2-, 3- and 4-irons. Beyond the fact that these clubs have less loft built into them, they're smart choices, even for shots in the 150-yard range, because they force you to make a controlled swing. In general terms, the more softly you hit the ball, the less actively the ball will spin. And since you usually don't want backspin on the low shot, it's wise to take plenty of club and keep your swing quiet.

The low shot is a great weapon in the wind because both a tailwind and a headwind will knock it down still further. A tight lie is a good place from which to hit a low shot, but a fluffy lie or a nest in the rough is not. Don't expect to be able to keep the ball down when you're standing uphill, but do expect a low shot from a downhill lie.

High shots are very difficult to play from hardpan, tight lies and fairway bunkers but relatively easy from perched lies in the fairway or from light rough. A strong headwind will tend to increase the backspin and height on a high shot, sending it almost straight up, whereas a strong tailwind will have a flattening effect. Finally, just as a downhill lie encourages a low shot, an uphill lie will naturally help you to get height, as you catch the ball more on an upswing than normal.

Meaningful Practice

Of course, the key to mastering both the basics and subtleties of shotmaking is practice. At some tournaments, people will come by and watch me practise, and I'll look to them like a complete hacker. First I'll hit a big slice, then, with the very next ball, a big hook. Then I'll hit one way up in the air, and without changing clubs I'll hit a low screamer. I'm simply practising my shotmaking.

To my mind, this is the most enjoyable practice of all. And one of the nicest things is it's good training for your visualisation and mental discipline as well. What I like to do is pretend I'm playing a particular golf course, and, using one club, such as a 4-iron, I try to hit the shots the course calls for.

If the first hole is a dogleg left, I'll try to hit a fade. If the hole normally plays into the wind, I'll try to hit a low second shot. Then I'll play the second hole, hitting a high downwind drive. I'll pretend that the flagstick on that hole is on the back left of the green, and I'll play a draw that will seek out the pin. I'll hit each of these shots with the 4-iron, hitting to a wide-open practice range. It's the ultimate test of your ability both to imagine shots and to play them.

The other great way to practise your shotmaking is to take a bag of golf balls, and toss them into some of the worst places possible – into fairway bunkers, behind trees, on to difficult lies. Then try to get the balls out of those positions in at least *two* different ways. If, for instance, you're blocked by a tree, try to hit a high shot over it as well as a draw or fade around it. This type of practice is, after all, the real thing. It also forces you to develop your imagination. Knowing how to hit these shots is of comparatively little value if you can't recognise the opportunities to play them. So get used to your talent at bending the ball, and test the limits of that talent. Once you know what you can and can't do from various lies, you'll 'see' shots you've never seen before. It's the combination of that talent and vision that will enable you to play aggressively from almost any lie.

I Dare You

Make the Ball Suck Back

There's an old story about the budding golfer who asks the old pro how he can get more backspin on his 5-iron shots.

'How far do you hit your 5-iron?' asks the pro.

'About 110 yards,' says the pupil, to which the pro replies, 'Then why do you want to make it come *back*?'

The fact is, if you hit your 5-iron only 110 yards, you do not have the strength or ability to make your iron shots spin back. If, however, you can hit a 5-iron at least 160 yards, then that suck-back shot which you've undoubtedly seen me and other pros hit on television or at tournaments is within your capability.

It's a wonderful shot to have, particularly when you're playing hard greens, or when you need to get close to a pin that's positioned just beyond the lip of a front bunker. And the way I see it, if I can spin the ball back, I have a big advantage on my opponents – they can only make the ball go in from the front of the hole while I can use the front door or the back!

The gallery loves to watch these shots, and I admit that I do too. One of my favourites came in the Italian Open a few years ago. They were offering a Lamborghini Countach that year for the first player who could make a hole in one on any of the par-threes. When I teed off for my second round, no one had done the deed.

At the second hole I hit an 8-iron that landed fifteen feet past the pin, took one hop and sucked back straight into the hole. Boy, was I excited. Fast cars are one of my greatest loves, and I had never driven a Lamborghini.

Well, when I got to the clubhouse, I was informed that a young Italian club pro had aced one of the other par-threes ten minutes before I had made mine. That $100,000 car had pulled out of my pocket just as quickly as it had arrived. And what did I get for making the *second* ace? A leather carry-all!

But I still have the memory of that hole-in-one, and of countless other shots that I've been able to hit into or near the hole because of an ability to apply extra backspin.

To play the shot, you need to have a combination of factors working in your favour, only one of which is your swing. First, it's absolutely vital that you have a firm, clean lie. The ball can be sitting on tightly clipped fairway, on hardpan, even on a good lie in a bunker, but that's about it. Don't even think about making the ball back up from the rough.

Secondly, the shot should not be a long one. Since you need a fair amount of loft, don't try this shot with any club longer than a 7-iron. Thirdly, the green should be firm – not hard like a pavement, but firm. If it's hard, you'll be lucky to keep any shot on it. If it's wet, the ball will just plug. What you want is a green that is soft enough to accept the shot yet firm enough to let the spin take effect. It also helps if the green slopes towards you. If it slopes away, you'll have no chance of backing the ball uphill.

Wind conditions also play a part. The shot is much easier when played into a wind. A headwind will increase your backspin. But don't try it in a tailwind, which will propel the ball forward.

Finally, be aware that certain balls and clubs enhance your ability to apply backspin. Any wound golf ball, or any two-piece ball with a cover designed to give maximum backspin, is better than any solid-centre or hard-covered ball.

The new box-grooved irons also allow you to put some extra spin on the ball. With these clubs a good player can make the ball stop dead even from the rough.

So if you have the ideal equipment working for you, you have a clean lie, and you're hitting upwind at a firm green that leans in your favour, your chances of backing up your shot are very good. Now all you have to do is hit it.

That, I'm afraid, is easier said than done. Basically, backspin comes from handspeed through impact. The harder and more crisply you can apply the club to the ball, the faster you'll make the ball spin back.

It's also important to hit slightly down on the ball. One of the reasons I'm able to apply so much spin is that I have a fairly upright swing which enables me to hit down rather steeply on the ball. When I want to, I'm able to make impact with the top-back quadrant of the ball. I actually squeeze the ball down against the turf, applying enormous friction and backspin. I don't take much of a divot, it's more like a crease in the turf or a slickening down of the grass.

To get this sort of impact, you have to play the ball back in your stance a bit. But not a lot. Some people think you should position the ball well back, as you would for a punch or low shot. That, however, just produces another low shot that may skid and stop; it won't suck back. Instead, you have to play it just a bit farther back than normal, so that you can pinch the ball rather than crashing down on it. My best advice is to experiment with your ball position a bit. When that pinch begins to be a smother, you'll have the ball too far back.

You must grip the club more firmly for this shot, because although it demands fast hand speed, it doesn't require a lot of wrist action. The swing must be aggressive with the entire body. Keeping the wrists firm, swing forward forcefully with your arms and lead through impact with your legs and lower body moving towards the target. Strive for that pinching impact, with as little divot as possible.

After a while you'll know by the feel of the hit whether you've put 'juice' on the ball. It's a great feeling and a great sight to see the ball land past the pin and come back close to the hole.

One other tip on this shot, something I learned on the final hole of the 1986 PGA Championship. Bob Tway and I were tied when we came to that hole. After he put his second shot in the right-hand bunker, I saw a chance to birdie the hole for victory. From a good lie in the fairway, I hit a wedge shot that landed next to the hole but had so much backspin it sucked right off the front of the green and into the collar of rough. Bob went on to hole that miraculous bunker shot for a birdie of his own, and with my ball in the thick grass I had almost no chance of tying him.

So take a tip from someone who has learned the hard way. When you have all the conditions going for you, take enough club to land your ball *past* the pin.

One reason I get lots of backspin on my shots: on my middle and short irons, when I'm swinging well I actually make impact with the top-back quadrant of the ball, pinching it against the turf and thus inducing lots of friction and spin.

CHAPTER 6

Not So Rough

HANDLING THE HEAVY GRASS

Learn to like the rough, because it's not going to go away. You'll be hitting into it – and out of it – as long as you play this game. Besides, it's not as bad as most people think. In fact, with the right attitude and the right technique, you can hit the ball longer and straighter from the rough than from anywhere on the course.

Indeed, the longest iron shot of my life may well have been a *5-iron* I hit one day from the rough. I was playing in the final round of the 1980 Australian Open at the Lakes Golf Club near Sydney. I had a one-stroke lead when I came to the tee of the 17th hole, a par-five. The fairway on this hole is an island, calling for something less than a driver off the tee.

I hit a 1-iron, and hit it too well. It went through the far end of the fairway and settled on a grassy downslope just inches from the water. From there I had 260 yards to a green with water on the left and worse trouble everywhere else. With a downhill lie I didn't want to mess with a low-lofted club, so I resolved to lay up short of the green with a 5-iron.

Well, as so often happens, in trying to put an extra-smooth swing on the ball, I nailed it dead-flush. The minute I felt impact I knew I had hit it big. It jumped out of the rough and flew forever. It did not land short of the green, it did not land on the green, it sailed clear *over* the green, leaving me a full wedge back to the pin. In all, that 5-iron travelled more than 300 yards.

I hung on to win that Open by a stroke over my countryman, Brian Jones, and a few months later I was amused to read a letter to the editor in one of the US golf magazines. It was from a fellow who had seen a description of the tournament. He couldn't believe the reports of my shot, and he ended his letter with an exhortation to the Australian Tour: 'Send us this man who can hit 300-yard 5-irons.'

I had trouble believing that 5-iron myself. But therein is a lesson. Expect the unexpected in the rough. Whereas 99 per cent of fairway lies are predictably alike, in the rough every situation is an adventure.

The Basics

Flyer Lies

Most lies in the rough are known as 'flyers', because of their tendency to produce shots such as that 5-iron of mine. What happens is that the blades of grass get between your clubface and the ball at impact, inhibiting your ability to create friction and apply backspin. The ball shoots out of the lie. With no backspin to pull it down, it flies higher and farther than a crisp fairway shot and it hits the ground running.

Virtually every time your ball nestles into light, dry rough, you have a flyer lie. The first thing to remember is to use less club than you would for a fairway shot of the same distance. If from 170 yards you'd normally hit a 5-iron fairway approach, go down to a 6-iron and maybe even a 7-iron from the rough. (The new box-grooved irons being sold by several manufacturers minimise the flyer effect, particularly for stronger players, but even if you have such clubs, you should take one club less from flyer lies.)

However, this advice comes with one caveat. Although the ball will jump off the clubface of your middle and short irons, and to some extent off the lofted woods (5, 6, 7, etc.), you won't get the flyer effect from the long-shafted steep-faced clubs. They simply aren't able to get down and through the grass. The truth is, you'll hit the ball about the

The main adjustment in handling flyers is to play the ball behind its usual position in your stance.

This will encourage the necessary downward attack that will minimise the intervention of the grass between your clubface and the ball.

same distance from the rough with a 4-iron as with a 2-iron, maybe farther. As a general rule, in fact, I would recommend that you do not attempt to play from a flyer lie with any iron or wood numbered 1, 2 or 3.

Your technique on this shot should be geared towards minimising the intervention of the grass. In other words, you want to hit the ball as cleanly as possible. To do that, you need to move the ball back in your stance. If, for instance, on a 5-iron shot from the fairway you position the ball off your left heel, move it back to an inch to the right of the heel for a shot from the rough. This ball position should leave your hands slightly ahead of the clubface at address. From that set-up you'll tend to swing the club up a bit more vertically on the backswing and return it a bit more steeply to the ball. With this steeper attack the clubface will come down on the ball rather than brush through the grass.

This single change in ball position is all you need to handle a flyer. Just make your normal swing as if you were in the fairway. There's no need to swing any harder or softer or to make any special movements or manoeuvres. Just trust your golf swing and apply it confidently to the ball. Remember, if you make reasonable contact with this shot, it will fly far and straight.

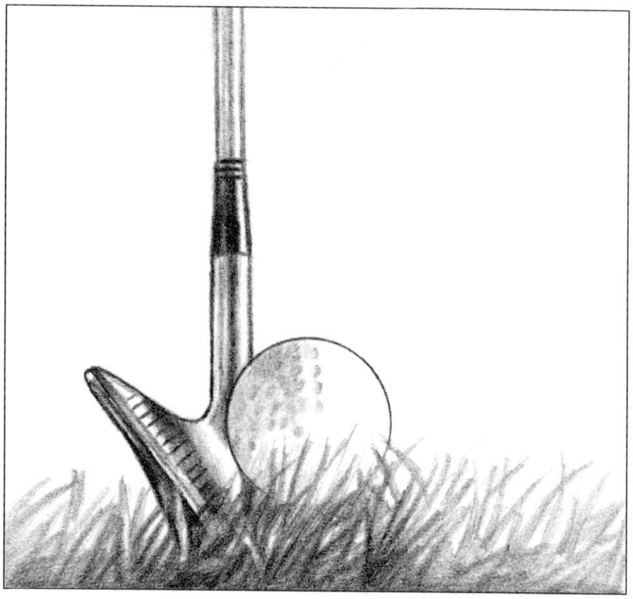

Any time your ball settles into light, dry rough you have a flyer lie, which will produce an essentially spinless shot that travels farther than a crisply struck ball.

Thick Lies

When you find your ball nestled deep in thick rough, you don't have a flyer. In fact, the best you can hope for from this situation is a sort of floater. Dense grass will slow down your clubhead to the point where you'll be barely able to extricate the ball. Whereas the flyer takes off like a rocket, this floater ascends like a blimp.

Your club selection on this shot is restricted to the short irons – 8, 9 and the wedges – with the pitching wedge usually the best choice. Once again, play the ball back in your stance, but this time play it two inches back instead of one, because you're going to have to go down and after the ball. To increase the steepness of the swing further, open your stance a few degrees, so that your feet, knees, hips and shoulders align to the left. Your clubhead should align square to the target line. It's the same basic alignment as for a slice, but when playing a short iron from the rough you won't have to worry about any sideward spin.

Since the grass will grab at your club and close the face at impact, you'll want an extra firm grip in your left hand. Alternatively, you can aim the clubface a bit right of your target at address, thereby allowing the grass to turn the face into a square position at impact.

The swing should be an aggressive, forceful one. If you get a kick out of swinging hard, this is the place to enjoy yourself. It's a powerful, steep chop that must go down and through the thick stuff. Be sure to keep the club accelerating through impact; otherwise you'll risk moving the ball only a few feet. The faster you can get the club moving through the ball, the faster that ball will climb out of its nest and the farther it will go.

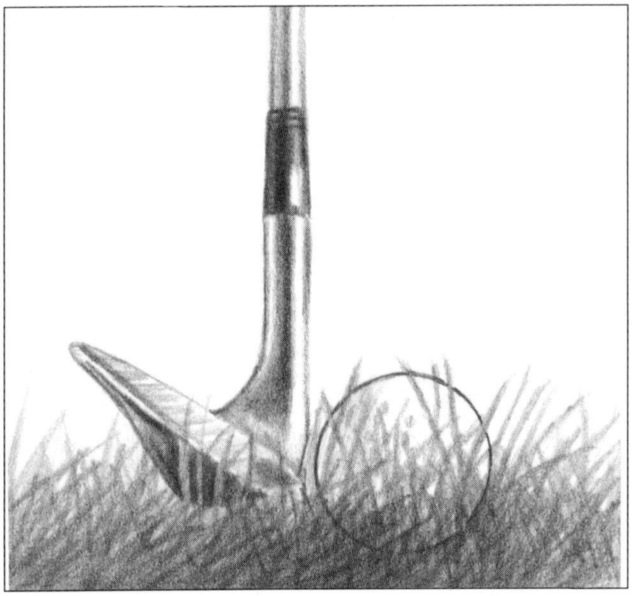

When the ball drops deep into thick rough, the best you can hope for is to excavate it with a sort of floating shot.

A perched lie, with the ball sitting up on the grass, looks easy to hit but demands careful attention.

Perched Lies

The final, and least common, rough lie is the perched ball, where you come to rest atop a tuft of grass. These lies appear easy but they're not. They invite you to belt the ball 200 yards, but you'll never *belt* it 200 – you have to pick it.

More than any other shot from heavy grass, the perched lie demands care and precision. Before you do anything else, take a close look at the lie to determine the exact level at which the ball is perched. In so doing, tread softly and be careful that you do not dislodge the ball, or it will cost you a one-stroke penalty.

Once you know the height of the ball, select your club. Generally speaking, you should take more club than you would for a fairway lie of the same distance – a 5-iron shot from the fairway would become a 4-iron shot from the rough – because of the tendency to hit slightly under this ball and come up short. Whatever club you use, be sure that you grip down on it an inch or so, so that you compensate for the fact that the ball is high off the ground.

Even if you don't normally follow my technique of addressing the ball with the club held slightly off the ground, do so on this shot. If you ground the club, you might disturb the grass beneath the ball and set off a chain reaction which will topple the ball. Also, if you address this shot with the club soled, you'll probably hit under it, maybe even whiff it. To hit the back of this ball you need to address your club to the back of it.

On the swing your single objective should be to take the club back in a low, wide sweep. To promote this, position the ball about an inch forward of its usual position in your stance, thus shading your weight a bit more to the right than on a standard shot. Also, be sure that at address your left shoulder is markedly higher than your right. Then just sweep the club back and away. Keep pretending the ball is on a tee, and you'll do fine.

The Aggressor's Edge

The basic types of rough lies are the three I've described. The actual number of situations you can encounter is limitless. For this reason, playing out of the rough is both an art and a science. Mechanical technique is important and so is power, but you also need some feel and finesse.

First, you should know whether you have the type of golf swing that handles rough with ease or with difficulty. Generally speaking, golfers are either hitters or pickers. The hitters tend to swing down and through the ball forcefully. It's a type of swing that can cause accuracy and consistency problems, but in the rough it's unquestionably an asset. Indeed, with this steep angle of attack, almost every rough lie becomes a flyer. If you have this type of swing, you may not even have to change your ball position except on the most deeply buried lies.

If, on the other hand, you tend to swing more flatly, clipping the ball off the grass with little or no divot, it's a different matter. With your picking motion, you won't get down and into the grass as much as a hitter will, so on some lies in light rough you'll have a choice. You can use your picking swing and play the shot with the same club and technique as you would a fairway shot, or you can play it back more in your stance, thus creating the downward hit that will, in effect, turn the lie into a flyer. Just be aware that when the grass is even the least bit dense, you're best off playing it as a flyer.

Regardless of what type of swing you have, some flyers fly more than others. In many instances, it depends on the direction in which you're hitting. If the grass is growing in the direction of your shot, you'll probably have a superflyer. The ball will really shoot out of this type of lie, so be sure to take at least two clubs less than usual. If, however, you're hitting against the grain of the grass, the ball can react as if it were buried deep. When you see this type of lie, play the ball back a bit farther, as you would for the buried lie.

Dry rough is more apt to produce a flyer than is wet. When thick grass is wet, you'll have trouble getting the club through the ball, so you'll get more of a floater reaction. Be aware, however, that when clipped *fairway* grass is wet, the ball will behave just as a flyer in the rough, since the water will get between the club and ball and strip the shot of backspin just as the long blades of grass do.

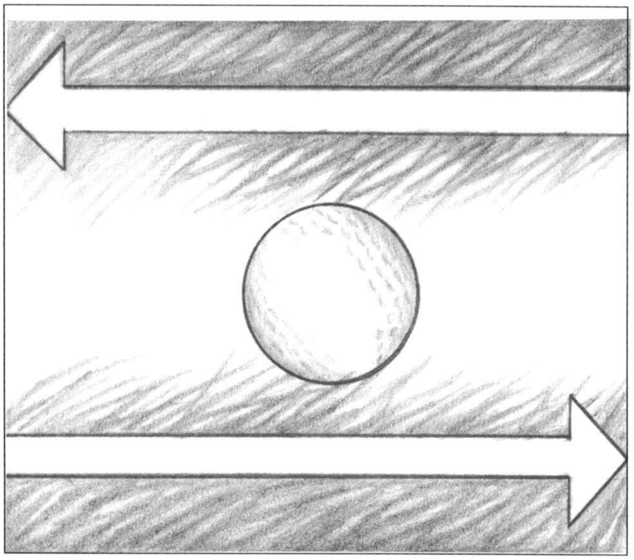

When the grass grows in the direction of your shot, expect extra flyer effect and take at least two clubs less than you would for a fairway shot of the same distance. When you're hitting against the grain, be ready for plenty of resistance. Be sure to play the ball well back.

Even on dry fairways you can occasionally get a flyer lie. On hilly courses, the mower blade tends to miss some of the dips and hollows, the very places that a golf ball tends to find. So be aware that flyers can come from position A as well as from the boondocks. Finally, be aware of the type of grass you're up against. Bermuda grass, found mostly in the southern tier of the United States, is much tougher and more wiry than any of the rye, bent and bluegrass strains. The worst thing about bermuda is that the ball always drops straight to the bottom. The most severe rough of this kind I've ever seen was in the 1984 PGA Championship at Shoal Creek Golf Club near Birmingham, Alabama. During one practice round that week I hit a ball into the rough one foot to the left of the 12th green. We never found it.

Playing out of bermuda takes an extra firm grip and an equally firm swing. Blue cooch, a grass found mostly in Australia, is also tough, as is the African grass called kikuyu. The worst thing about kikuyu is trying to play little pitch and chip shots out of it. It's impossible to bounce a ball through that stuff. Indeed, I've seen guys flop a pitch shot into kikuyu fringe grass and have the grass actually throw the ball back at them.

One smart thing to do before taking on any rough lie is to make a couple of perceptive practice swings. Find an area of the rough that's similar to your lie, and take a few swipes at it, noting the amount of resistance you get as you come through the grass. I can't tell you how often I get surprised when I do this. Invariably, the grass is either less or more tough than I thought it was. When the grass is easier than I thought, I'll usually switch clubs and go to a shorter stick. When the grass is tougher than I thought, I'll either take a more lofted club or I'll play the ball a bit farther back, firm up my grip and make a harder swing.

The most important aspect of playing from rough is to continue to play aggressively. Too many people – particularly those with the 'picker' type of swing – are intimidated by grassy lies. You have a lot of things going for you, assuming you follow the basic techniques I've outlined. So don't be afraid to be aggressive, no matter what the lie. Remember, there's more distance and accuracy built into this spinless shot than in any other. Remember also that when you're in a situation that requires a lot of height, light rough is the best place to be. If, for instance, you have to loft the ball over a tree, your chances of doing it are actually better from a flyer lie than from the fairway.

From a flyer, don't listen to the people who say you can't put the ball on the green. Granted, you may not be able to hold the green with a shot from the rough, but in many instances all you have to do is allow for the ball to *bounce* on to the green. Aim for the centre of the widest opening to the green, and land the ball just short of it. (If the fairway is hard and dry, land it well short.) Even when you have to clear a bunker, your chance of holding the green will not be that poor from a flyer lie, particularly when you have a 7-iron or less in your hand. With the added height you'll be getting, the ball will descend more vertically than from the fairway. It won't have much 'bite' but sometimes its stopping ability will surprise you.

From floater lies, everyone tells you to take your medicine and go quietly. The traditional advice is to accept the loss of a half stroke or so and to wedge the ball back to the fairway. That may be true in the very worst of situations, but I say you can go for distance from many of the thick lies.

The key is to pull the ball. We've all made the mistake of taking too little club and then swinging too hard. The result is a dead pull to the left. It normally goes the full distance, pin-high or beyond, but it finishes several yards left of the target. Well, the idea on the buried lie is to play that shot intentionally. The next time you're in one of those situations, put the pitching wedge back and go with the 9-iron, the 8-iron or even the 7-iron. Play the ball well back, as you would for any deep lie, but aim yourself a few yards right of the target. Then make the firmest swing you can while still maintaining good balance. The faster moving clubhead can usually get through the grass with less resistance, and the result will be something between a floater and a flyer that will jump out to the left of where you aimed it. You'll surprise yourself – and your opponents – at how long you can hit this shot.

Even the perched ball can – and should – be played aggressively. In fact, when you have 200 yards or more to the green, I suggest you hit this shot with a driver. A driver from the rough? Absolutely. In fact, I think it's the smartest choice. It has the deepest face of any club in the bag, and that means you'll have the least chance of whiffing underneath the ball. And its long shaft encourages you to swing back low to the ground, which is exactly what this shot demands.

I Dare You

Play a Seven-Fingered Shot

One of the most frustrating aspects of playing from the rough is the fact that it's difficult to develop any finesse. Particularly around the green, it's tough to make the ball land softly and stay near the target.

Recently, however, I developed a shot that can do some tricks. The idea originally came from one of the masters of touch, Seve Ballesteros. While practising sand shots with me one day, he taught me something I've since adapted to the rough.

Let's say you want to hit a high, soft shot over a bunker and make it stop near the pin. That's a tall assignment from the rough, but with this technique, it's possible. After setting up for a high shot, make a normal swing, but just before impact, release the pressure in the last three fingers of your left hand. You don't really let go of the club, but you do lighten that pressure down to almost nothing. The result is that your right hand flips through and under the left, flipping the clubhead under the ball and upwards. At the end of the shot, the bottom of the club faces straight towards the sky. The shot flies very high, comes almost straight down and sits tight after it lands.

The seven-fingered shot: to make the club flip upwards through the ball, lighten your left-hand grip pressure as you swing through impact.

In early 1987, at the A.T. & T. National Pro-Am, sizing up my approach for a chip to the green.

On the golf course I talk to my caddie constantly. It keeps me focused and psychologically reinforced.

Left. *At Turnberry all the work, all the determination came to fruition as I reached my goal of winning a major championship.*

Without question, the best golf tactician I've ever seen is Jack Nicklaus. He always selects the smartest shot.

Over-aggressiveness got the better of me at the 72nd hole of the 1986 Masters.

Practising for the M.C.I. Heritage Classic, Hilton Head Island, South Carolina.

Occasionally you'll find yourself in a predicament where none of the traditional escapes will work. It's a desperate shot, but if you analyse and approach it intelligently, you'll maximise your chances of pulling it off.

The 1987 US Masters. To my mind, the most important shot in golf is the drive.

One of the keys on the low shot is staying in front of the ball at impact. It follows, therefore, that when you want to hit a high shot you should make adjustments that will allow you to stay behind the ball.

Since the grass will grab at your club and close the face at impact, you'll want an extra firm grip in your left hand. Aim the clubface a bit right of your target at address, thereby allowing the grass to turn the face into a square position at impact.

The chip shot is a miniature swing controlled by hand–eye coordination. And the coordination has to come first.

Left. *Once you develop a good bunker game, you'll immediately reap several benefits. First, you'll shave a shot or two off your handicap. Second, it'll have a positive effect on your long game.*

Good green reading comes with experience. After hitting enough putts over enough different types of terrain and grass, you develop a sixth sense of how the ball will roll. As you walk on to a green, whether you realise it or not, you take in all sorts of subtle information.

On the fairway woods and long irons, the differences from the driver are minor. The clubs, after all, are nearly as long as the driver. The resulting swings are therefore similar to the big, wide sweep for a teeshot.

CHAPTER 7

Learning to Love Sand

BUNKER PLAY

I wish I had known Walter Hagen. From what I've read and heard, he was a man after my own heart. He went at life – and golf – full bore. Hagen wasn't a classical stylist, but he had tremendous self-confidence, and when the heat was on, he knew how to get his ball into the hole.

The Haig had a few good one-liners too, and one of my favourites relates to bunker play. 'The sand shot is the easiest one in golf,' he said. 'After all, it's the only one where you don't have to hit the ball.'

That may be a bit whimsical, but the attitude is right. When Hagen swaggered into a bunker, he was ready to play a great shot. Most of the guys on the pro Tour feel the same way. In fact, they'll tell you they'd rather play from sand than from heavy grass.

Most amateurs, however, are just the opposite. When they step into a bunker they're scared to death. If you're one of those people, you have a big problem – and an even bigger opportunity.

You have an opportunity to join one of the most elite fraternities in the game. Think about it. The world of golf is full of great putters and long drivers and deft chippers, but how often do you come across a truly fine sand player? You have an opportunity – and an easy one – to surpass millions of golfers – simply by becoming sharp from the sand.

Once you develop a good bunker game, you'll immediately reap several benefits. First, you'll shave a shot or two off your handicap. Secondly, it'll have a positive effect on your long game. If you don't fear bunkers, you won't tend to steer your drives and approaches away from them, and you'll make a more free and confident swing. Finally, in match play a good bunker game will be a tremendous psychological weapon. Every time you get up and down from the sand you'll give yourself a boost while giving your opponent a jolt.

Believe me, I've felt both. After two holes on the Sunday of the 1986 British Open I held a three-stroke lead over Tommy Nakajima, with whom I was paired. But my approach to the third green landed deep in the left-hand bunker, seventy-five feet from the pin. With Nakajima safely on the green, it looked as if at least part of my lead would disappear, unless I could get that ball close. Well, I didn't get it close, I holed it for a birdie. Nakajima then three-putted for a bogey, and suddenly my lead was five strokes, the eventual margin of victory.

Less than a month later I lost the PGA Championship when, on the 72nd hole, Bob Tway, with whom I was tied, blasted out of a greenside bunker and into the cup for a victorious birdie.

So I've been on the up and down sides of bunker magic. I'm sure you have too, and I'm sure you'll agree that it's more fun to be on the up side. So let's quit talking about great bunker shots and start learning to play them.

The Basics

Sand play is elementary physics. I was never a science whiz in school, but I learned enough to know that if you push the sand in the correct manner, it will transfer your energy and lift the ball in the way you want it to fly. It's basic earthmoving.

Let me be specific in an area where I *am* comfortable – in the water. Think about splashing around in a pool. When you want to splash someone way on the other side of the pool, you whisk your palm across the top of the water with a flat, skimming motion, creating a long, low wave. When you want to splash someone right next to you, you slap downward on a sharp angle into the water, for a high, cresting wave.

Picture a golf ball riding the tops of those splashes, and you'll have a good idea of the basic forces at work in bunker play. Instead of water, your ball rides out on sand. Instead of using your hand to make waves, you use the club.

The Right Sand Wedge

The type of club you use is important. I'm constantly surprised at the number of amateurs I encounter who carry no sand wedge at all; they simply play bunker shots with a pitching wedge. Unless you're a very talented golfer, this is like trying to eat soup with a fork.

The pitching wedge, like all the other irons, has a thin leading edge that digs down into the sand. The sand wedge looks sort of like a pregnant pitching wedge because the back-bottom of the blade bulges out in the form of a flange. This flange is often referred to as 'bounce', because that is what it mades the club do on impact with the sand.

Just as the hull of a speedboat bounces along the top of the water, so the flange of the sand wedge bounces off the undersurface of a bunker. As it does, it creates that wave of sand which lifts the ball out of the trap. So be sure that you get a sand wedge that has adequate bounce. You don't want a huge flange – that could cause you to bounce up so quickly that you belly into the side of the ball. On the other hand, you don't want a thin-flanged wedge because it will dig in just as surely as a pitching wedge. If you're in doubt as to the precise amount of bounce you should have, talk to your PGA professional.

Four 'Musts' on Bunker Shots

Once you're adequately armed with a sand wedge, be aware of a few things that need to be done when you address virtually any bunker shot.

1. *Get good footing.* Grind your feet firmly into the sand. This will help promote a solid stance and good balance. It's also a way of doing some detective work, to determine the texture and consistency of the sand. Since the Rules prohibit you from grounding your club in a bunker, you should try to learn as much as possible about the lie as you take your stance.

2. *Choke up about an inch on the club.* When you grind your feet down into the bunker, you bring your hands closer to the ball. You need to slide them down the grip, or you'll tend to hit well behind the ball and dig too deeply into the sand.

3. *Open your stance.* Most bunker shots require a steep downward attack on the ball; an open alignment, with the feet, knees, hips and shoulders pointed well left of the target, will facilitate this type of impact. You'll need to open up various degrees for the different shots, but 90 per cent of bunker shots are played from the open stance.

4. *Don't keep your eye on the ball.* Instead, watch a spot about an inch to an inch and a half behind the ball, since that's where your impact should be. Don't hit the ball on this shot: the spot is never on the top of the ball.

With those four basics you'll have a tremendous start at solid bunker play.

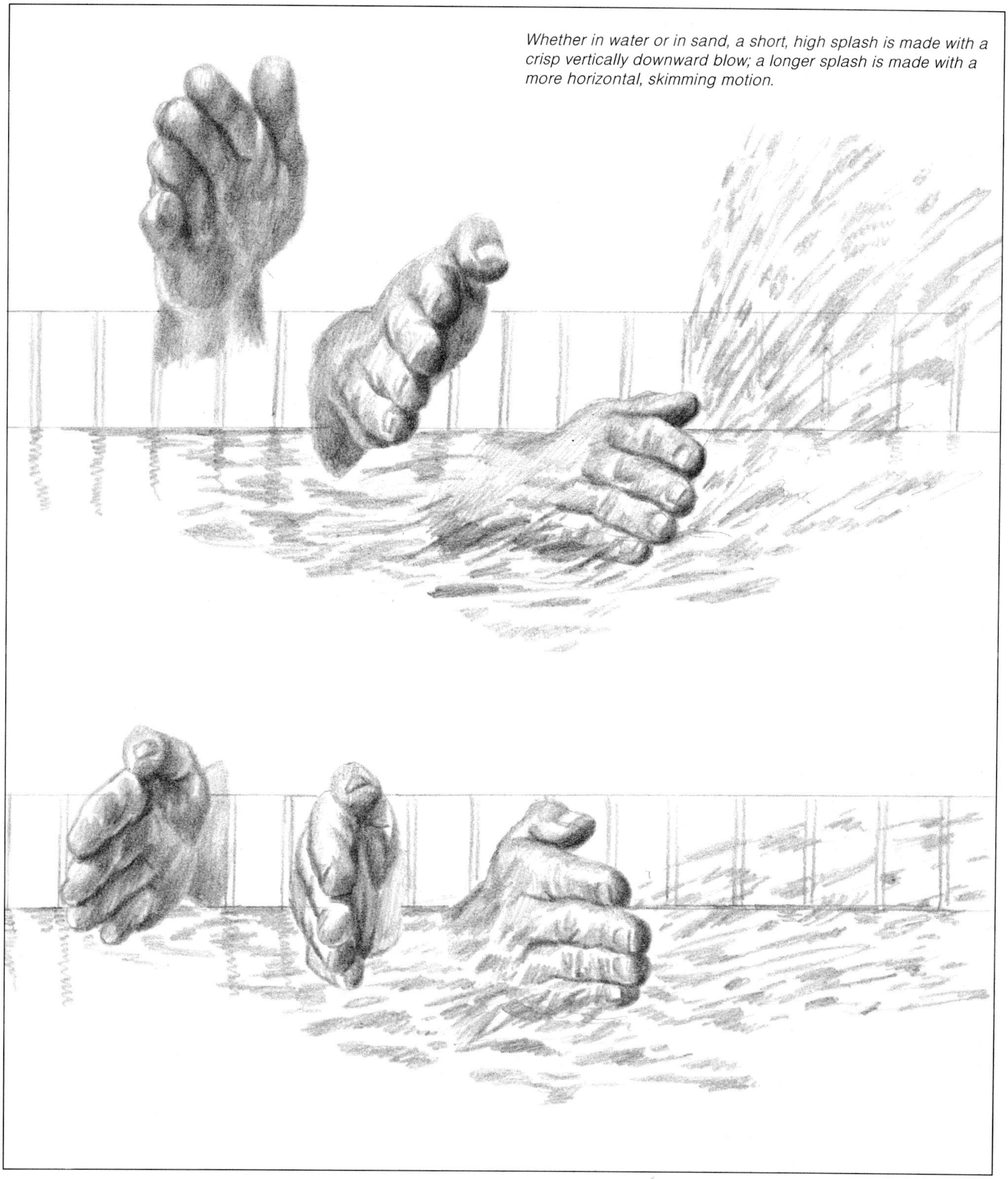

Whether in water or in sand, a short, high splash is made with a crisp vertically downward blow; a longer splash is made with a more horizontal, skimming motion.

Every bunker shot requires firm footing – don't be afraid to grind your spikes well into the sand.

I have four bread-and-butter shots from greenside bunkers – the runner, the one-bouncer, the stab and the softee. Each serves a different purpose.

The Runner

When I have plenty of green between me and the pin, I play the ball back in my stance, about midway between my feet, with my stance slightly open. The clubface is open and laid back – it's aiming a couple of feet to the right of the target with the face pointing almost skywards. (When you lay the clubface back, don't let it touch the sand.) This address sets me up for a quick upward movement of the club that must be initiated by an early cocking of the wrists. The downswing is simply an unhinging of the wrists, as the club swings down into the sand at that point about an inch or so behind the ball, then bounces upwards into a full follow-through. Get your club out of the sand and up into the air, if you want the ball to do the same.

The One-Bouncer

If I need to fly the ball to the flag, I'll play my one-bouncer, which is basically a long, high version of the running shot. The set-up is the same as

Grip down on the club for increased feel and control.

An open stance promotes the vertical up-and-down movement that greenside bunker shots require.

Don't *keep your eye on the ball. Instead, focus on a spot just behind it, where you want to penetrate the sand.*

for the runner – open, laid-back clubface, open stance – but I do make a change in the ball position. Instead of playing it back in my stance, I'll position it up off my instep. This will encourage me to hit the shot on the upswing, adding the necessary loft. When I play this shot properly, the ball arcs into the air, flies to within a few feet of the green, takes one bounce and sits tight. This is basically the sand version of the long splash in the swimming pool.

On the swing I concentrate on keeping everything slow and rhythmic. Just before I take the club away from the ball I tell myself, 'Slow back, slow through.' Since the ball is forward, you won't tend to pick up the club as wristily as for the runner, and that's fine except when you have to clear a high lip. In that case, open both your stance and the clubface a bit more, and make your takeaway a little more wristy and vertical.

The last part of this shot may be the most important – be sure to finish the swing and raise the club

The runner: play the ball midway in your open stance and make a short backswing but a full, forceful move through impact.

up into a follow-through. Then you accelerate through the ball and impart the necessary energy to lift it out of the bunker and across the green to the flag.

The Stab

I love the stab shot. It's a terrific way of getting out of a heavy lie, where the ball sits semi-buried in the sand. It's particularly useful when you don't have much green to work with, because it produces a soft, floating shot rather than the fast, scooting one that normally emerges from this type of lie. (This is the sand version of that short, high water splash I mentioned.)

Again, set up in the open stance, this time with the ball about midway between your feet. Open the club several degrees, even if your ball is plugged in the sand. (Traditional instruction advocates playing heavy lies with a square clubface, but I find that

too limiting. If you swing at this shot aggressively, you'll get the ball out just as easily with an open face, and you'll get that soft landing.)

The whole key to the stab shot is the stabbing swing itself. The backswing is the usual wristy movement with the hands going to about shoulder height. But on the downswing you slam the club down into the sand and *leave it there*. In fact, it's almost a hit-and-recoil type of action, as if you were stabbing something with a knife and quickly snatching back the blade.

With the clubface well open, you'll penetrate the sand with the heel end of the club, and if you stab down with sufficient force, you'll displace the sand in such a way that it will bump the ball softly upward. The longer the shot you need to hit, the less open your clubface should be.

The stab: use a well-open clubface, and slam it down into the sand with little or no follow-through. The ball will pop up softly.

The Softee

My final bread-and-butter shot is the softee, and for this one I'm indebted to my friend and fellow competitor, Seve Ballesteros. This is in fact the seven-fingered shot I mentioned on page 112. I developed it for play from grass after Seve showed me how he used it in bunkers.

It was during the week of the 1983 US Open at Oakmont that I noticed Seve playing some practice shots, in a bunker on the edge of the 18th fairway. He was making the strangest swings I had ever seen, even for the innovative Ballesteros. He seemed to make a sort of underhand release, flicking the club upward at impact. It looked weird, but it produced the softest little sand shots I'd ever seen.

'What the hell are you doing?' I said as I stepped into the bunker.

'It's a secret,' said the Spaniard with that playful smile of his. Then he graciously shared that secret with me.

You use this shot from a good lie when you need to make the ball climb quickly and stop soon after it hits the green. Once again, take the open stance and open clubface, and this time position the ball well forward, off your left instep. Make the wristy, vertical pickup, but on the downswing, loosen your grip with the last three fingers of your left hand. This will cause your right hand to take over and flick the club under the ball and upward, raising it sharply into a high, floating flight.

Be careful on this one. When you loosen your grip it's easy to let the club get caught in the sand, and that can defeat the purpose of the shot. It's vital that your hands accelerate through the ball at good speed. For that reason, never try this shot from anything but a good lie.

The softee: it's the seven-fingered shot from sand. Loosen your left-hand grip pressure at impact, and watch the ball float upwards.

The Aggressor's Edge
Developing a Sand Player's Sixth Sense

Sand play was one of the last aspects of golf I took seriously. It was not until after I started playing the US Tour regularly that I really began to work on my bunker game. Oh, I had a grasp of the basics but no real finesse, no sharpness. I guess I was so cocky in those days that I figured I'd rarely have to dirty my spikes in the sand.

Boy, was I naive. After a couple of years of watching guys like Gary Player and Seve Ballesteros I realised I'd never be a complete player – or a consistent winner – without a strong bunker game. So I worked on the refinements, using the bunker as my laboratory and experimenting with all sorts of nuances of stance and swing.

I learned a couple of important things. First, I saw that there is more room for artistry and creativity in a bunker than in any other corner of the

The best favour you can do yourself is to spend a couple of serious hours developing your own feel for the sand.

course. You have so many options, so many ways of playing a shot. And the more options you know, the more confident and aggressive you can be.

Secondly, I saw that bunker finesse is far easier to develop than putting feel or a soft touch around the green. Why? For that same reason Walter Hagen mentioned – you don't have to hit the ball. The sand acts as a buffer, a margin for error. And therein is another source of confidence, another reason to play bunkers the only way they can be played – aggressively. Until you can make firm, confident swings and actually try to sink that ball out of the sand, you won't be going at these shots with the proper attitude.

I emerged from that learning period with the four basic shots I've just outlined. But I don't suggest that you adopt all four. You might find it easier to play only two types of sand shots – or you might be able to use six or seven. My point is that you should go through the same type of experience I did and feel out your own arsenal of shots. The best way to learn sand play is to teach yourself, by relating different set-ups and swings to the corresponding ball flights and rolls. In this way, you'll develop your own sixth sense in bunkers.

What you'll learn, more than anything else, is the way to vary the length and trajectory of your shots. There is a greater variety of opinion on this subject than on almost any other aspect of golf instruction.

Some teachers and players advocate that, to increase the length of a sand shot, you should simply increase the length and force of the swing. Others say it's merely a matter of increasing or decreasing the distance you hit behind the ball. And still others key on ball position and weight distribution.

My own practice sessions have put me in the 'vary the amount of sand' camp. I've spent hours hitting balls, thousands of sand shots – and hundreds of those swinging with my left hand only, to get a feel for the way the club reacts with the bunker – and I know that one thing is unarguable: the more sand you take behind the ball, the less backspin you'll apply, the lower the ball will fly and the longer it will run. Conversely, the less sand you take, the more backspin you'll apply, the higher the ball will fly and the faster it will stop.

Related to that law of the desert is another law: the more open your sand wedge at impact, the less sand you'll explode and the more height and backspin you'll put on the shot; the less open the face, the more the club will dig down into the sand and the less height and backspin you'll get.

Combining these two laws will help you to play virtually any shot you'll encounter. For instance, if you want maximum height and bite, the idea is to turn the clubface as open as possible and take as little sand as possible, by hitting right next to the ball. (Indeed, if you can make impact so that just a few grains of sand intervene between your club and ball, you'll have the ultimate in friction and backspin. In a sense this is like hitting the ball with a sandpaper-faced club – as you can imagine, it produces maximum backspin and bite. When you see me or other Tour players make the ball suck back from sand, this is what we've done – we've played a wide-open-faced shot and we've taken just a thin veil of sand with the ball.)

Looking at it another way, this is the reason that a ball always runs a long way when it's hit from a buried lie. When the ball is buried, you have to go down after it. To get down after it, you have to dig into the sand, which means a square face. Digging down deep means that you'll be taking a lot of sand with the shot, which produces a low ball that runs a mile.

The suck-back shot and the buried lie are two extremes. More often, you encounter a situation that's somewhere in between, and typically that means a compromise in your technique. For instance, the ball is semi-buried, but you don't have the luxury of hitting a hot-running explosion, because you're near the front lip of the trap and the pin is fairly close to you.

It was for situations such as this that I developed the stab shot – an open face combined with a hard downward dig into the sand. The open face gives me the height and bite, the downward dig gets the ball out.

Attacking the shot with an open clubface will produce a shallower cut of sand and a high shot with lots of backspin.

Other players have developed other solutions. Creative guys like Ballesteros and Chi Chi Rodriguez have dozens of different sand shots. Jack Nicklaus played for years with just two basic shots he called the explosion and the splash. As I said, the best way to solve the mysteries of the sand is to take the basics with you into a bunker, learn how the physics of earthmoving affect ball flight, and develop a set of shots that fits the course you play most often, and fits your overall game.

Knowing the basics of sand play takes away your fear; knowing the subtleties will actually lead you to enjoy playing from bunkers. Once you have a feel for these things, you can pursue some of the finer points of bunker play, adapting your technique to different types of sands and the challenges of uneven lies.

Adapting to Different Sands

In the course of my yearly tournament schedule I see a half-dozen different varieties of sand, each with a different degree of coarseness, compaction and depth. Each of them calls for a slightly different attack.

Call it chauvinism if you want, but I've always felt that the finest bunker sand in the world is in Australia. Maybe I'm just used to it. After all, for a decade or so before I became a golfer, I spent a

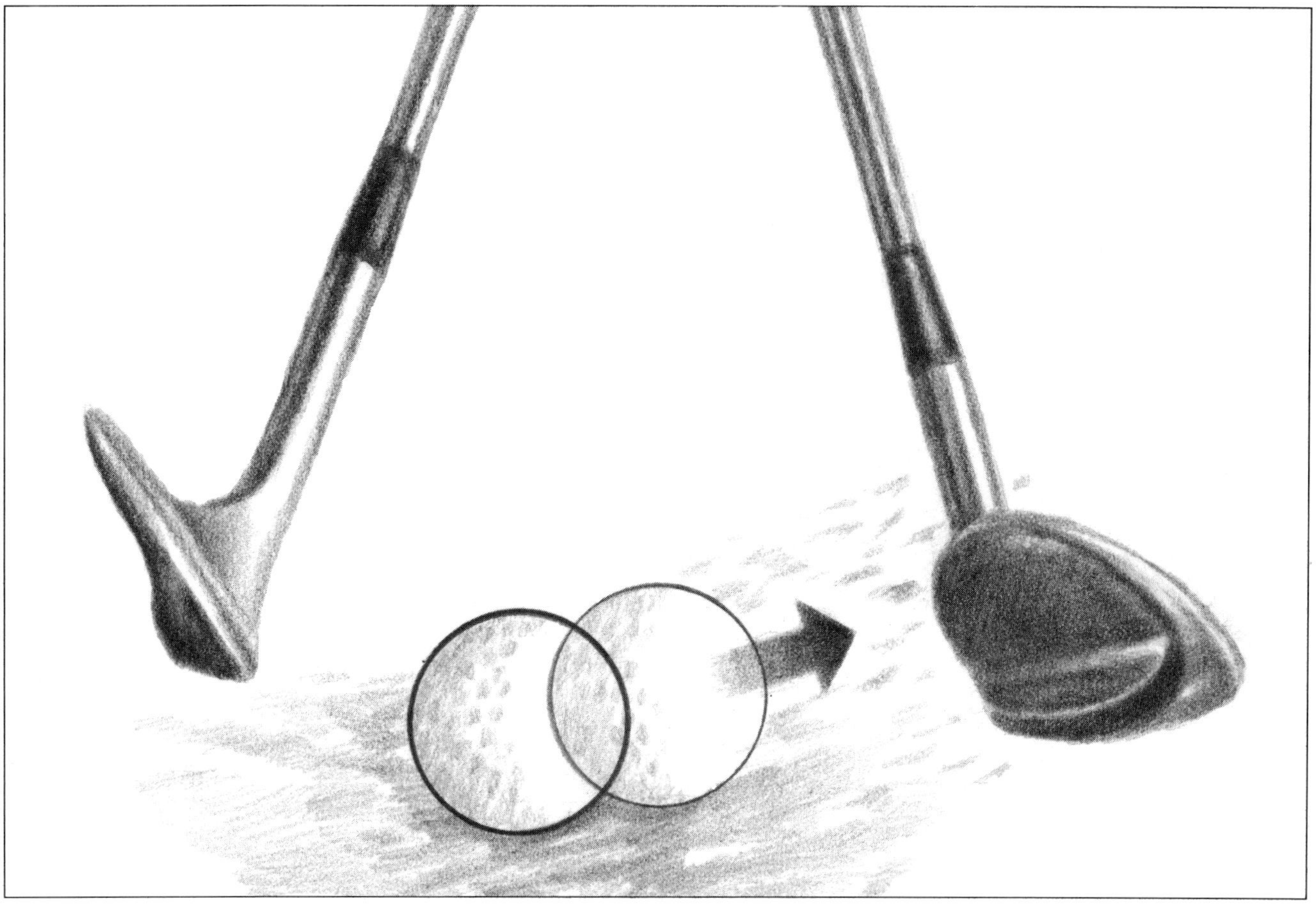

A square-faced attack will dig into the sand more and yield a lower, running shot.

lot of time on the Australian beaches.

The Aussie sand is rather granular and firmly packed, and the bunkers at most courses are shallow-based and constructed so that the ball rarely plugs, even in the front lip. Instead, it just rolls back down the face.

The same type of sand is prevalent at many of the British courses, certainly at the seaside links where beach sand is smoothed and compacted by constant wind. (Consequently, buried lies are relatively rare in the British Open.)

In general, this type of sand is easy to play from because you can judge more easily the chain reaction from club to sand to ball. You can also impart plenty of spin from these firm bunkers because you tend to get a lot of bounce. For that reason, you should generally attack such shots with a less open clubface than you would use in most bunkers. It's also wise to play the ball back in your stance a bit more than usual. This will encourage a more digging action and guard against a belly-bounce.

In deep, powdery bunkers such as those at the Augusta National and Oakmont, the wedge will tend to dig and bury. So it's wise to play from these bunkers with a well-open sand wedge and to position the ball a bit more forward in your stance than usual. The loose consistency also requires a relatively firm swing. If you play most of your golf on a course with this type of sand, you should be sure to get yourself a wedge with plenty of flange.

The trickiest kind of bunkers may be those with loose sand over a firm crust. When Bob Tway holed his explosion to beat me at Inverness, he played from this type of bunker. In hard-bottomed bunkers such as this the ball rarely buries, but you have to be careful nonetheless. Generally, your club will glide smoothly through the sand and ball, unless you dig a bit too deeply and cut into the crust. When that happens the club can slow down, causing you to leave the ball in the sand. It's safest to attack these bunkers with a heavy-flanged wedge, to allow the club to bounce off the subsurface.

I like to play out of the British bunkers because the sand is often wet. This packs it together densely, providing a uniform cushion under the ball so that the wedge slides smoothly underneath and bounces up and through rather than digging deep.

Uphill lie: plant your right foot firmly, align your shoulders with the slope, and take slightly less sand than you would from a level lie.

In wet sand, you usually have a clean, unburied lie, and this tempts many players to try to play out with a chip shot. As far as I'm concerned, that's absolutely the worst idea in the world. As aggressive and confident a player as I am, I never try to play chip shots from the sand. The margin for error is simply too small. In fact, I'll take out a putter and roll the ball out of a bunker before I'll chip it.

Another reason never to chip from wet sand is the fact that a blast is so simple. You actually have a couple of options on how to handle it. If you need distance, you can address this ball with a square face, since from wet sand you don't have to worry about digging too deeply. And since the wet, compacted cushion will transfer your energy quickly, you don't need to swing very forcefully to get plenty of fly and roll. Just take the usual open stance and make a smooth pass at the ball, hitting an inch and a half behind it.

If on the other hand you need to play a short shot to a tight pin, this is your chance to show off, maybe even make the ball suck back into the hole. Open the face of the wedge wide and lay it back, position the ball just back of centre in your open stance, and make a very quick, nipping swing – short back, short through but with plenty of acceleration – taking only an inch of sand behind the ball. Go at this shot with confidence. When you hit it properly, you can really make the ball dance.

Hilly Lies

One of the most testing bunker situations – no matter where you're playing – is the uphill lie. This shot often appears easy, with the ball sitting on the upslope waiting to be hit, but it's easy to misplay.

The main point at address is to set your shoulders parallel with that upward slope, so that your swing can follow a relatively normal path. Your weight should be shaded on to your right side so that you'll swing the club up the slope rather

Downhill lie: play the ball well back in your stance, open your wedge wide, and make a hard hit down and through the sand.

than into it. Firmly plant that right foot as you settle into your stance.

One mistake amateurs often make in this situation is to play the ball well forward in their stance. That's a good idea from uphill lies on turf, but not in sand, because you risk hitting the shot too high, and possibly leaving the ball in the sand. For this reason, I play the ball in about the same position I do for most bunker shots, just off the left heel.

The clubface is slightly open as usual. The swing is upright with a lot of hand and wrist action. Since you'll tend to drive this club into the face of the bunker at least a little bit, you should take a little less sand behind the ball than you would from a level lie. Also, because the tendency from an uphill lie is to leave the ball short, it's particularly important on this shot to make a firm swing and follow through, to get the club up and out of that slope of sand, and raise the ball upwards along with it.

I think the most difficult sand shot of all is the

downhill lie from the back lip. It's a tough lie to begin with, often made still tougher when you have to play with your right foot out of the bunker.

Still, there's no reason to give up, as many people do, chipping out to the side or hacking at the ball desperately. As with the uphill shot, begin by aligning yourself parallel with the slope. Play the ball well back in your stance, nearer to your right foot than your left, and get your hands well ahead with most of your weight on your left foot.

You'll need plenty of loft to get this ball up and over the lip, so open the face of your wedge wide. Now, if you remember your laws of the desert, that open wedge means that you won't dig up much sand. But your assignment is complicated on this shot, because in order to get that ball up and out, you really have to get the club down underneath it. Therefore, on this shot, more than on any other, you'll have to pick the club straight up and slam it straight down forcefully with your hands, striking

Ball below your feet: widen your stance, flex your knees and bend markedly from the waist, to ensure that you stay down to the ball. Make a controlled arm swing.

the sand a little closer to the ball than normal. Just be sure to hit *down* hard, or that open-faced wedge will surely bounce out and you'll blade the ball either into the face of the bunker or clear over the green. Resist the temptation to try to lift this shot out – that's the surest way to a big score.

I faced this type of lie several years ago during a practice round at the Masters. On the par-three 12th hole my teeshot buried in the back bunker, leaving an impossible downhill shot across the fast green, with water on the other side. In truth, I had no shot at all, but I figured, what the heck, it was a practice round. So I let loose a crashing swing, and somehow the blade of my wedge caught the edge of the ball just right.

The ball squeezed up the clubface with a terrific amount of spin, then shot out low, straight across the green. It looked for sure as if it was headed for the water when, just as it reached the hole, it stopped dead, as if by magic. I think it was still

spinning around when I marked it. Hale Irwin, who was playing with me at the time, said it was the most incredible golf shot he'd ever seen. Frankly, I've tried to duplicate that shot on several occasions, and I've never come close.

The sidehill bunker lies also are tricky, but with a couple of adjustments you should be able to handle them. When the ball is below your feet, the idea is to 'get down' to it at address and stay there during the swing. Therefore, you must grip the club at the very end, let out the shaft. Also, flex your knees more than usual, and bend a bit more from the waist as well.

The ball should be positioned midway in your open stance, and your clubface should be slightly open as usual, but since there's a tendency to push the ball to the right from this type of lie, align yourself a few yards to the left of your target. In effect, this will result in your clubface aiming straight at the hole. Give yourself a particularly firm footing in the sand on this shot, and try not to let your weight get off your heels.

From that position, make a wristy three-quarter swing with as little leg action as possible.

When the ball is above your feet, you have to guard against digging into the side of the bunker face and taking too much sand. Choking up a couple of inches on the club will help protect against this.

The tendency from this lie is to pull the ball to the left, so set up with the ball midway in your stance and aim a bit right of the target. This time, don't grind your feet in too deeply – that would just put you that much more below the ball, making the shot even tougher. So wiggle your feet in just enough for good balance, with your weight shaded slightly towards your toes. You'll need a relatively forceful swing on this shot, but not a long one, so a short, quick up-and-down action is best.

Remember, it's just as important on bunker shots as anywhere else to visualise the shot before you hit it. See the ball floating out on its spray of sand, arching over the lip of the bunker, landing on the green and rolling up to the hole. Maintain this mental picture as you address your shot. This will blot out the mechanics, erase any fear or doubts, and allow you to play your bunker shots with the feel, confidence and aggressiveness they require.

I Dare You

Slice an 8-Iron

Here's one of the greatest shots in the game – and a wonderful way to handle golf's toughest situation, the long bunker shot.

Usually, when you have forty yards or more to the pin, it's a matter of playing a long version of either my runner or my one-bouncer shot. These can be tricky to gauge, even for pros. The problem is, to get enough distance with a sand wedge you have to take a fairly big, fairly hard swing while also minimising the distance you hit behind the ball. Even the best golfers occasionally make the mistake of coming a bit too close to the ball and blading the shot, or of quitting on the downswing and fluffing it entirely.

For these reasons, I've developed a secret weapon for long bunker shots – a slicing 8-iron. You can't use it when you're facing a buried lie or a high lip, but in all other cases I'd recommend it over the long explosion.

Take the 8-iron and don't choke up on it – use the full length of the club. Play the ball well forward, off your left instep and take a very wide, very open stance. You should aim yourself more left than on any other shot, about 45 degrees or so. The clubface, like your stance, should be open, and laid back as well.

What you want to do is make a shallow, splashing explosion. You won't have to worry about getting too deep because the ball is well forward in your stance and the club is well open. Still, the idea is to hit at least an inch and a half behind this ball, and that's a lot of sand for a long shot. The longer shaft and stronger loft of the 8-iron will help you get distance, but you still must give this a hard swing. However, that's what's nice about this shot – you can belt it and you don't have to worry about digging down deep; and you can get all the distance you need without having to hit too close to the ball.

But the best part is watching the ball dance. When you hit this shot right, it'll fly on a line several yards left of your target, hit the green still at least ten feet left, and then suck directly back to the right. When you apply that sandpaper-like friction to the ball, this shot will scoot to the right faster than any shot in the game.

It takes some practice – all sand shots do – but once you get a feel for it, you'll find yourself relying on this slicing 8-iron to bail you out of the toughest of predicaments. And you'll amaze your friends at the same time. Yes, this is a shot Walter Hagen would love.

CHAPTER 8

Attacking the Pin From a Hundred Yards In

THE SHORT GAME

Believe it or not, I played golf for thirteen years and won two dozen tournaments worldwide before I ever learned how to hit a chip shot. No kidding. Up until 1983, I was just plain lousy around the green.

At first I didn't realise it. Hell, back in Australia I hit most of the greens and putted like a demon. Who needed a short game? Even during my years on the European Tour I got by basically on sheer strength and good putting.

It was when I joined the US PGA Tour that I got my comeuppance. In event after event I played myself into strong contention, and then blew it when I failed to pull off a crucial finesse shot. Before long the American press noticed my greenside stumbling, and I started to get a reputation as a gorilla, a guy who could hit the ball hard but didn't know how to hit it soft.

I hated those articles, those comments. I hated them because I knew they were true. So at Christmas in 1983, I decided to turn things around. I decided to teach myself touch.

Off I trooped one morning with my pitching wedge and a big bag of balls to the practice green of the Grand Cypress Resort near my home in Orlando, Florida. I started by hitting chip shots and trying to analyse what was wrong with my technique. Before long I found it. I had a hitch in my swing.

I was hitting my chips with a double wrist-cock. I'd break my wrists going back, and then, at the end of my backswing, I'd cock and uncock the wrists again, leading to a sort of delayed-hit chip shot where the clubhead lagged behind. It's similar to the move Don January makes on his full swing, a kind of buggy-whip action at the beginning of the downswing. That move has worked beautifully for Don's long game, but it was ruining my short game.

Having determined my problem, I set about finding a cure. I'm not sure why, but the first thing I did was drop my pitching wedge and pick up a handful of golf balls. Then I started tossing the balls to one of the holes on the practice green. Cupping each ball in the palm of my hand, I swung my arm slowly back and slowly through, releasing the ball on the forward swing.

I must have tossed five hundred golf balls that day, and with each toss I think I developed another nerve ending's worth of feel. By the end of that day I had learned more about the short game than I had during the entire previous thirteen years. Today, I rank my chipping and pitching among the major strengths of my game.

The Basics

Above all, my one-day education taught me this: the chip shot is a miniature swing controlled by hand–eye coordination. And the coordination has to come first.

Now, granted, some people are born with better hand–eye coordination than others. Even among the pros, there are some guys who can do all sorts of parlour tricks, bouncing the ball off their clubfaces and so forth, and other guys who can't. But even if you don't have this ability, you can develop a feel around the greens, just as I did – by tossing golf balls.

It's actually kind of fun. The fact is, I still practise this way from time to time, just to stay in touch, so to speak. And you'll often see me at a tournament, tossing an imaginary ball when I'm trying to determine how to handle a tricky greenside shot. I'll usually do it from two places – once from the landing spot of the pitch or chip, then once from the ball.

So take a dozen balls or so, pick out a spot and start tossing. (If anyone laughs at you, tell them

A marvellous way to develop hand–eye coordination for chipping is simply to toss golf balls to targets on a practice green.

The ball should not be held in the fingers. Instead, cup it in the palm of your hand.

You'll find that the basic motions for the toss and the chip are very similar.

you're just doing the same thing Greg Norman does all the time.) Throw high balls and low balls and try to make them stop as close to your target as possible. Watch the way your tosses perform – how they fly, how they react when they hit the green, how they roll to the pin. Throw real high ones that fly all the way to the hole and sit, and low ones that run almost like putts. Throw to some tough positions too, bouncing the ball across humps and knolls to get to the target. Make some downhill tosses and uphill tosses, and see which kind of flight and roll works best for each.

What I learned is that, for 99 per cent of chip shots, the 'low road' is smartest. Whether you're tossing a ball or hitting it with a golf club, it's much simpler to feel and control a rolling shot than a lofted one.

Therein I discovered another weakness of my old technique. Basically, I used to chop at the ball and hit a rather high chip shot. Now, I keep the ball low, using a method developed directly from those practice tosses.

The Chip Shot

When tossing the ball, I had to face my palm directly at my target. I also had to swing my arm straight back and through, and the only wrist action was a natural flex on the longer tosses. Those two elements – a square right palm and a smooth armswing – became the cornerstones of my short game.

But those are just two of the basics of the short game. In playing virtually any shot around the green, you need to make a few important adjustments in your set-up.

First, narrow your stance and open it up, so that your feet, knees, hips and shoulders are aligned about 20 degrees left of square, and your heels are close together. On a chip shot, your heels should be no more than six or eight inches apart. The narrowness will help you to minimise weight shift and body movement which can sabotage your touch and control. The open stance will enable you to get a good look at the target.

Second, grip down at least an inch on the club, and much more if you like. Sometimes, I'll grip down right to the metal if it feels right. Shortening the distance between your hands and the clubhead puts you in closer touch with the ball – almost as if you're tossing it – and that enhances your feel. Gripping down also enables you to take a good crisp swing without worrying about hitting the ball too far.

For a standard chip shot, your ball position

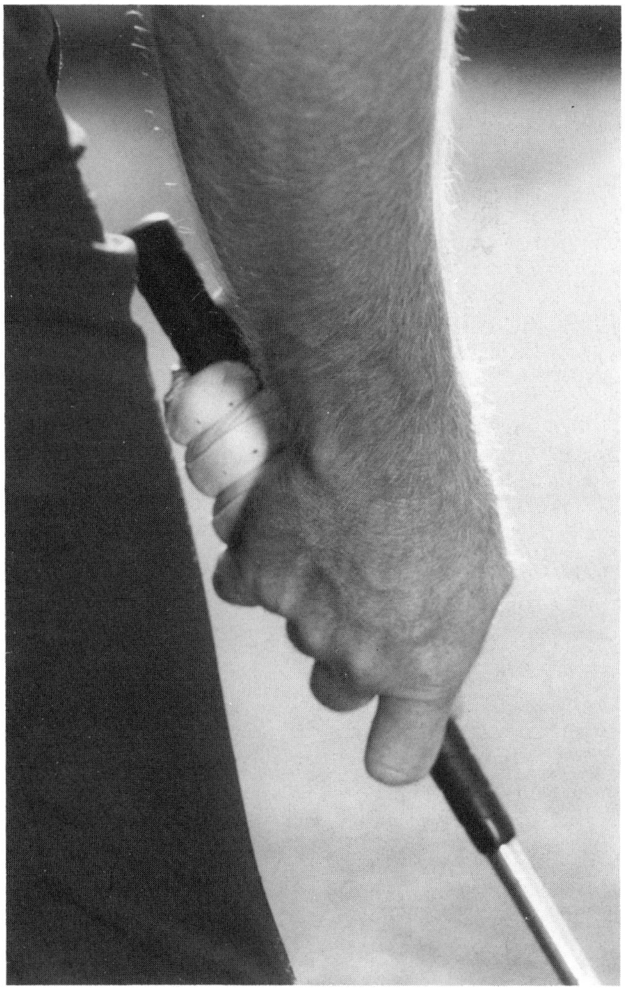

For virtually every shot within fifty yards of the green, you should choke down on the club. Shortening the distance between your hands and the ball enhances your feel – almost as if you're making a toss.

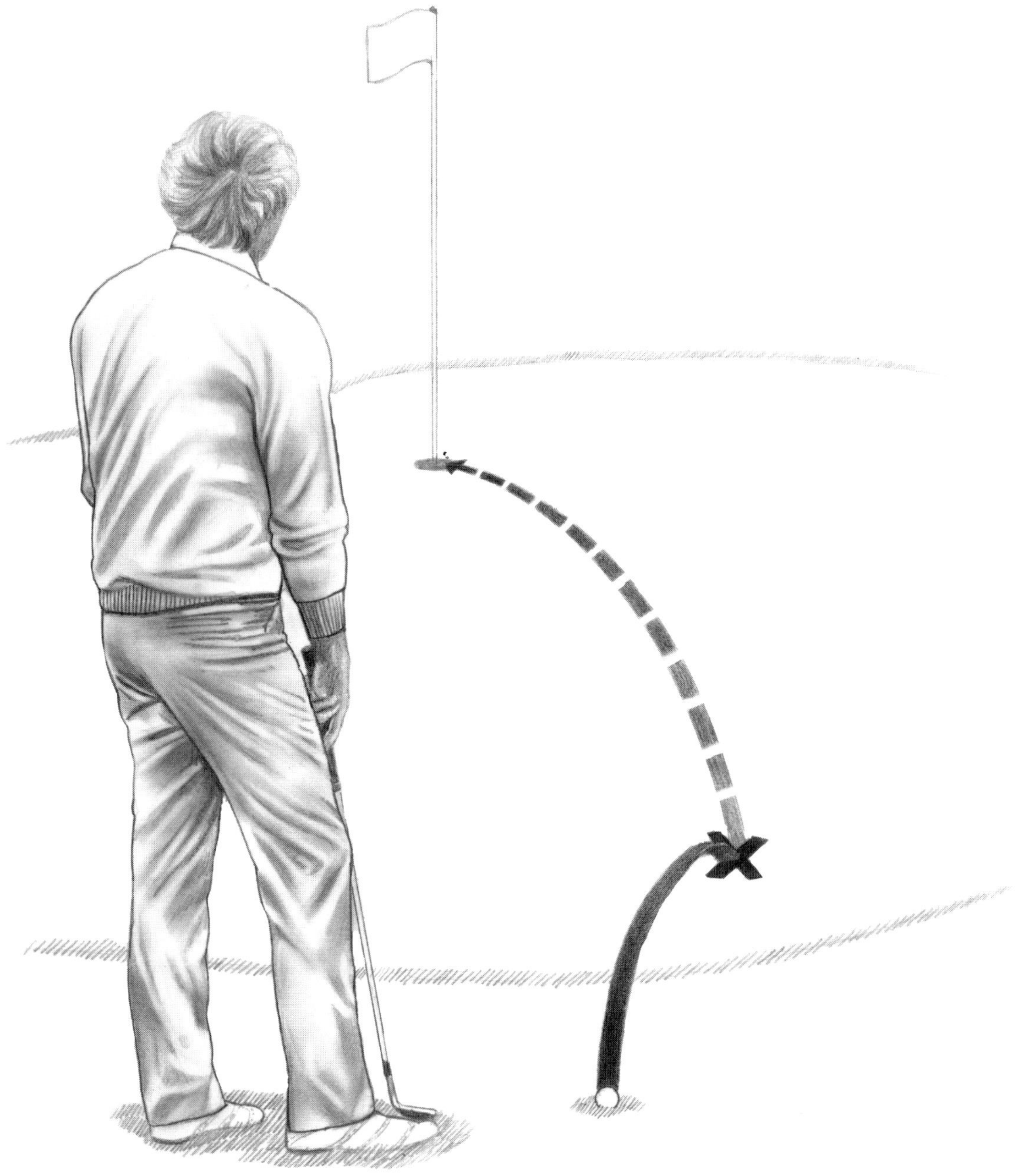

Chip shots require visualization too. See the ball landing on the green and making its roll to the hole. Then gear your thoughts and set-up towards making the ball hit that landing spot.

should be about the same as for a long shot, off the left heel or perhaps a hair behind that. With the open stance, however, it will seem as if the ball is farther back, and that's fine, because you want to have a bit more weight on your left side and you want to keep your hands ahead of the ball, both at address and throughout the swing.

As I said, the chip is basically a mini-swing. I don't try to do anything fancy or make any special moves. It's just a short backswing controlled by the arms. The longer the chip I have, the farther I bring the club back, but it's rare that my hands swing as far as waist height.

Ken Venturi, one of the game's finest teachers, advocates a completely wristless style of chipping, and Phil Rodgers, a short-game wizard, teaches an extremely wristy method. I don't agree with either of them, because neither method is natural. Each is trying hard to use a style.

To my mind, the chip shot is as natural a movement as tossing a ball. If your wrists break, they break, but don't try to keep them stiff and don't try to flick them. Let the wrist cock occur naturally. On the shortest of chips you'll have no wrist action at all, on the longer ones you'll have quite a bit, as the weight of the clubhead tugs on your hands at the end of the backswing. But for Pete's sake, don't think about it – just let it happen.

You can learn a lot about the overall look of the chip shot by watching Tom Watson. No one is better around the green, and a big reason, I believe, is that Watson hits his short shots *hard*. Tom is, by nature, just as aggressive a player as I am, and that attitude is reflected in his short game. Notice how he brings the club back briskly and returns it crisply to the ball. Using this compact up-and-down stroke, he's able to put plenty of backspin on the ball, for good control. He's also able to pop the ball out of the trickiest lies, and get it consistently up to the hole.

So be crisp and aggressive on even your shortest shots. Lead through impact with your hands, applying a slightly descending blow to the ball. One test, to be sure you're hitting the shot this way, is to imagine a race between your hands and the clubhead, with your left knee as the finish line. If your hands don't win that race every time, you need to work on your chipping.

The proper move through impact is to brush the top of the grass. In fact, it's always wise to take a couple of practice swings before you play a chip, and get the brush–brush feel of taking the club back through the fringe and bringing it through the ball. When I have a tough chip, I'll search out an area that simulates my lie and then go through this little dress rehearsal. Invariably, I'll learn something about the texture and resistance of the grass that will help me to adjust the force of my actual swing.

The final point in chipping is a strategic one. Concentrate on knocking the ball in the hole, but gear your shot-planning to a specific spot on the green. As you assess the situation, visualise the ideal shot – play it in your mind. This will show you the point at which the perfect shot will hit the green and begin its roll to the pin. Focus on that spot, and gear every bit of your technique to making the ball hit it.

In general you want to get the ball rolling as soon as possible, and this is where club selection comes into play. Some excellent golfers, Jack Nicklaus among them, play up to 90 per cent of their greenside shots with the same club. In Jack's case that club is the sand wedge. Other players prefer the pitching wedge.

To my mind, that's making things too difficult. It forces you to stretch the capabilities of the club – and yourself – too far. The way I see it, there are seven or eight golf clubs in my bag that are useful around the green, so why not take advantage of them? I play my chip shots with anything from a sand wedge to a 3-iron, depending on the demands of the situation. The more green I have to work with, the lower lofted club I'll use. For instance, when I'm on the fringe facing a chip of seventy or eighty feet, I'll take out the 3-iron and hit what amounts to a long putt. Using my normal chipping stroke I'll pop the ball just on to the putting surface

Reebok

and let it roll all the way to the hole. I'll also use the long and middle irons on uphill chips, especially when the ball has to climb to the top of a two-tiered green.

For a forty-footer, I might go down to a 5- or 6-iron, for a thirty-footer, an 8 or 9, and for the shortest chips I'll use one of my wedges. This way I don't have to try anything fancy or make any outlandish adjustments so that my club will fit the shot. I just use that same basic chipping swing, keeping the technique simple, consistent and confident.

The Pitch Shot

Add a few yards to the chip shot, and you'll be facing a pitch. Generally, chip shots can be from a few feet to about twenty-five yards. Beyond that, you're pitching.

The address for the pitch is similar to that for the chip – an open, narrow stance, the ball off your left heel, your hands forward and your weight shaded to the left side.

The difference is that everything is a bit less marked than for the chip. The stance is a bit wider – your heels will be about a foot apart. It's less open, too, with your body pointing only about 10 degrees left of square. You grip down about an inch on the club.

The swing is basically a long chipping swing. Obviously, you'll have some degree of that natural wrist action, but again, let it happen, don't make it happen. Keep your legs and lower body quiet and let the arms do most of the work.

There's a great variety of opinion regarding the best way to vary the length of pitch shots. Some teachers suggest varying the length of the swing, others advocate gripping up and down on the club, and a third philosophy says you should vary the pace of the swing.

Let me rule out that third alternative immediately. Except on the special shots which follow – the lob and the punch – I don't believe in changing the pace of the swing. You have a natural tempo, and unless a difficult situation requires you to change it, you shouldn't. As I said with regard to the chip, short shots must be struck aggressively, crisply. This leaves the two other methods – varying the swing length and varying the grip length. I use both of them. The shorter the pitch I have to play, the shorter the swing I'll use. And when I get down in close range, I'll grip down on the club as well. The key is to allow myself on each shot to make a firm, aggressive swing. I take length out of the club

As far as I'm concerned, half of the clubs in the bag are useful for chipping.

Generally speaking, a pitch is nothing more than a long chip where a fair amount of ground must be crossed before the ball reaches the green.

and length out of the swing in order to maintain a firm, confident attack on the ball.

On the shortest of pitches, I'll simplify things even more by switching from the pitching wedge to the sand wedge. Why grip way down and shorten my swing when there's a higher lofted club that will do that work for me? And today, with the advent of a third wedge with even more loft than the sand wedge, even the shortest of pitches may be made with a minimum of swing variation. The 60-degree wedge has about 5 degrees more loft than the sand wedge and about 10 degrees more than the pitching wedge. For playing the short, high shots that need to stop quickly, it's an amateur's best friend.

With any pitch shot, however, planning is vitally important. Pick out the spot where you want the ball to land. With a hard, fast surface that spot may be short of the green. On soft, uphill shots, it may be quite close to the hole. So give the shot some thought. Then take your practice swings as you

The pitch: using the same narrow, open stance as for the chip, make a slightly longer swing, allowing the wrists to hinge and unhinge naturally.

visualise the ball lofting to your ideal landing point. This will help you generate the right feel.

The Lob

Two variations on the pitch shot that everyone should know how to play are the high pitch, known as the lob, and the low pitch, commonly called the punch.

The lob is the weapon to use when you have to get the ball up in the air quickly – to clear a tree, a bunker, whatever – and make it settle quickly near the pin. It's most easily played with the 60-degree wedge, if you carry one, but may also be played with a pitching wedge or sand wedge.

Ball position is the main key. Since you want to get the ball up fast, you should position it up off your left toe. Your stance should be wider than on any other short shot, but still not quite as wide as for a full iron swing. Most important, you should

stand well open, aligned about 30 degrees left of your target, with your weight distributed equally between your feet. To get a feeling of being behind and under the ball, kick in your right knee just a hair. Finally, you should open the face of the club several degrees, and lay it back a bit. This will increase the effective loft of the club. The higher you have to hit the ball, the more open and laid back the club should be. Just be careful, when you use a sand wedge, that you don't build too much 'bounce' into the shot, especially if you're playing the ball off firm turf.

This is the only short swing that shouldn't be crisp and aggressive. In fact, the best swing for the lob is long and lazy. Assuming you aren't on hard-pan or a very tight lie (which would prohibit this shot) you want to slide the face of the wedge under the ball the same way you would on a bunker shot. Gripping the club a bit more loosely than normal will help put some smoothness into your swing.

The lob: Both the stance and the clubface are well open and the ball is up near the left foot, all to encourage plenty of loft. Grip the club loosely and make an ultra-smooth, lazy swing with a high finish.

Take your hands back to at least belt height and at most shoulder height, depending on how far you want to hit the ball. To ensure the proper pace of swing try to make your downswing the same speed as your backswing. You won't be able to do that, but if you come close, while maintaining acceleration through the ball, you'll have this swing mastered.

When you bring the lob shot off, it will land softly and dribble to a stop. From the tighter lies it will tend to kick to the right after its first bounce, so allow for that by aiming a bit to the left.

The Punch

The punch shot has saved me countless strokes over the years. In the 1986 Masters, the punch came to my rescue on the 71st hole, after my teeshot strayed under a tree. From there I had a little over a hundred yards to the green but the ball had to

fly under the tree limbs, then clear the rise of the elevated green and sit tight. One behind Jack Nicklaus, I couldn't afford to play cautiously.

Taking a 9-iron I smacked the ball just the way I wanted, and it came to rest ten feet away from the pin. When the putt went in, I had birdied four holes in a row. All for naught, as it turned out, since I bogeyed 18 to lose by a stroke. Still, it was gratifying to play such a good punch shot under pressure.

You can think of the punch either as a low pitch or as a long chip shot. It can be played with anything from a 7-iron to a pitching wedge – the 7-iron if you want it to run after it hits the green, the pitching wedge if you want it to stop.

Set up with the ball at least an inch behind your left heel, your hands well forward of the clubface, and about 70 per cent of your weight on your left side. Your stance can be square for this shot. Grip down a bit on the club, but most important, grip firmly.

The punch: at address, the ball is back, your hands are up front, your stance is square and most of your weight is on your left side.

From here it's a quick-back/quick-through swing with an abbreviated follow-through.

The swing is quicker than that for any of the short shots. What you want is a quick-back/quick-through motion with some snap to it. Keep your wrists out of it, and keep the clubhead as low to the ground as possible, both during the backswing and during the short follow-through. Standing a little open puts a bit of a fading tail on this shot. A slightly closed stance makes the ball draw just a bit.

Feel is important on this one. When you select your club, make trajectory your first concern, behaviour of the ball on the green your second concern, and distance your last. If the shot is a hundred yards, don't feel that you have to hit the wedge, unless you want the ball to stop quickly after it hits – a 7-iron will often do the job with less effort.

The Aggressor's Edge

Two words will do you more good than anything else I can tell you about the short game.

Get hungry.

Get hungry for the bottom of the cup. Because that hunger, that aggressiveness, is what makes the difference between a player who wastes strokes around the green and one who consistently turns three shots into two.

At the risk of offending the fair sex, I'll make an observation. In men's professional golf, nine out of ten players show this aggressive hunger. On the women's Tour nine out of ten do *not*.

Generally speaking, the lady pros score just as low as the men, but how many times do you see an LPGA player birdie the last couple of holes to win? Rarely. And when women pros get into sudden-death playoffs, what score wins? A birdie? Almost never. It's usually a par, sometimes even a bogey. The men players consistently get their short shots up to the hole, the women pros consistently fall short. A star such as Nancy Lopez stands out simply because she has the guts to go for the pin.

Sadly, most amateurs resemble those women more closely than the men. When they face a thirty-foot putt they may think about holing it, but when they face a thirty-foot chip, they just want to get up and down.

If that's your attitude, change it.

Change it because there's no reason you shouldn't play your short shots with all the skill – and confidence – of a PGA Tour player. You may never hit your drives as long as I do or make your irons stop on the green the way mine do. But with the basic short-game knowledge I've just given you, and the refinements I'm about to discuss, there's no reason why you shouldn't be able to go chip shot for chip shot against me or any other pro in the game.

All you need is the right attitude – the right focus. When I'm hitting a teeshot, my goal is a fairway forty yards wide. When I'm playing an approach I'm hitting to an area the size of a swimming pool. But once I'm inside 100 yards, I have only one target in mind – the bottom of that little round hole. Adopt this focus, and you'll take the first step to a sharp short game.

The second step goes back to that idea of teaching yourself touch. Once you have a good grasp of the basic short-game shots – the chip, pitch, lob and cut – start experimenting a bit. Go out to a practice green with your pitching wedge, and fiddle around with your set-up. Not your swing – your set-up.

Experiment with different ball positions – move it up in your stance, then back – and note how those changes influence the flight and roll of your chips. Then vary the openness of your stance and see what that does. Play around with the clubface too – open it as wide as you can get it, and see how high you can pop the ball. Then close it down and hood it and watch what that does to your chips.

Then back off a few yards and see what happens when you introduce these variations in your pitch shots. Watch the way each shot flies, and how it rolls – or stops – after hitting the green. Open your clubface and stance as far as possible and see how high you can lob the ball. Then close them down and see how low you can punch it with the same club. Get to know how all these changes produce different results, and you will give yourself a post-graduate degree in the subtleties of the short game.

What that knowledge will give you is freedom – freedom of choice. You'll be able to select your shots. One of the subtle things that separates people with touch from the rest of golfers is the fact that they always have two or three options. Players with only one or two greenside shots become victims of the golf course and have to stretch and force those shots to fit each challenge. But players with several options can take charge. Since they know how to play different shots and they know exactly how those shots will behave when struck from various types of lies to various landing areas, they can look at a situation, evaluate the options and come up with the shotmaking choice that offers the best chance of success. On the Tour, we call this playing 'dial a shot'.

I do this all the time. In fact, there was one time in 1986 that I had to dial and then re-dial a shot. It was on the last hole of the PGA Championship.

Bob Tway and I were tied, and with Tway in the bunker and me in heavy rough about fifteen feet short of the pin, I decided the best choice was a sand-wedge chip, to sort of pop the ball out softly and let it roll uphill to the pin. If it got to the hole, fine; if it didn't I knew I'd be a foot or two away. This was one time when I decided the best policy was to play for a cautious par rather than trying to jam the ball into the hole for a birdie. It's hard to be aggressive from rough, and I didn't want to leave myself a downhill putt. Besides, I figured that if I could cosy the ball within a foot or so, I'd certainly tie Tway for the Championship, and possibly beat him. After all, he might not get down in two from that bunker.

Well, my instincts were right in one sense. Bob didn't get down in two – he got down in *one*, with one of the most electrifying shots in major championship history. Suddenly, I had a whole new situation, calling for a whole new shot.

As the crowd at Inverness exploded, I walked over to my caddie, Pete Bender, and said, 'Let's let these people calm down and then we're going to have to reroute our thinking.'

My sand wedge went back into the bag, and out came the pitching wedge. Now, I had only one goal – to knock the ball into the hole and tie Tway. What had been a relatively easy chip shot for an up-and-down par had become a very difficult punch shot for birdie. I needed to gouge the ball out of the grass for a low, scooting shot and hope that it would come out straight enough and softly enough to slam-dunk into the hole.

I wish I could conclude this story with a fairy-tale ending, but as most golf fans know, my shot didn't go in, it went past the hole. Still, it was the right shot to play – the only shot – under the circumstances. I'm just glad I had the ability and knowledge to give myself that second option.

Difficult Lies

Once you develop your shotmaking options, it's simply a matter of knowing when and where to apply them. So here are a few of the commonest greenside challenges and the best ways of handling them.

From any sort of hardpan or firm lie, your best option is to punch the ball. The idea is to trap or pinch it, by pulling the club into the back of the ball, as you would for a punch. Any other type of swing might cause you to bounce the club off the hardpan and belly into the back of the ball. The same punch shot is best from a cuppy lie or a lie in a divot, where you have to go down and scrape the ball out. Play the ball back in your stance, and lead

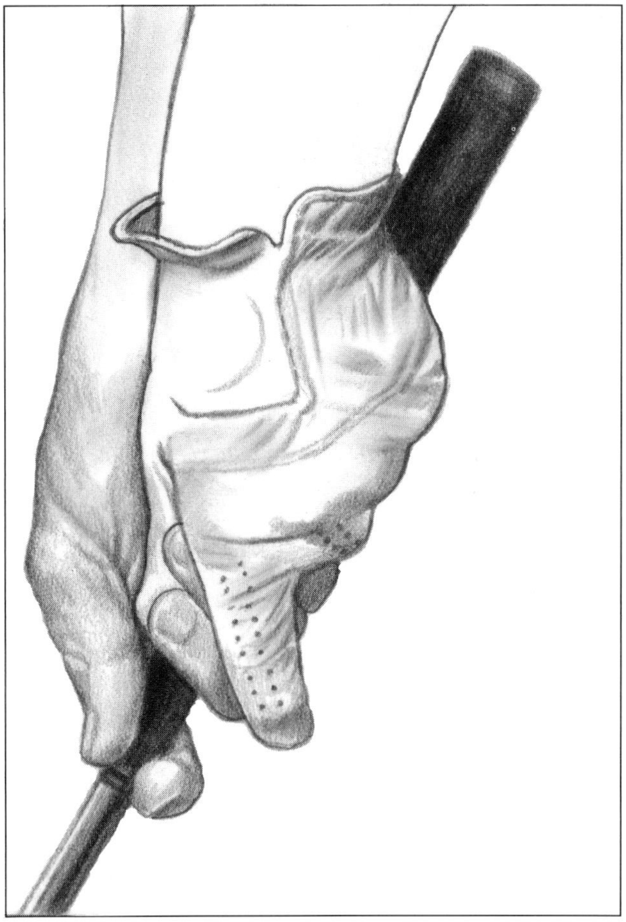

When I want to deaden impact for a short, floating type of chip, I'll use my putting grip – a reverse overlap – which minimises wrist action.

through with your hands into a low follow-through. These shots will not fly very high, and you can expect them to run a long way.

From the opposite type of lie – heavy grass – the ball can react in either of two ways. If you go at it aggressively, it will jump out fast, like a mini-flyer. If you play it with a soft, dead-handed swing, it will sort of float out. These were the two shots I was 'dialing' against Tway at Inverness. So if you want a shot that jumps out quickly, take a pitching wedge or 9-iron and play a punchy sort of chip, with the ball well back in your stance and a brisk, stabbing swing. If you want the floater, play it more like a lob. Move the ball forward in your stance, open your clubface a bit and take a slow, smooth swing.

If it's a short floater you want to hit, you might try a trick I like to use which helps me eliminate wrist action: I use my putting grip, a reverse overlap, with my left forefinger covering the first three fingers of my right hand. This, combined with an

The uphill chip: align yourself with the slope, and flare your left foot towards the target, as a brace. The most common error on this shot is to leave the ball short, so be particularly aggressive.

arm-and-shoulder swing, seems to deaden the impact. It's also a good technique to use from wet fringe grass where you won't get as much backspin as normal. The shot should be played with either a sand wedge or a 60-degree wedge.

When you have a lie in heavy grass and you need to move it more than a few yards, use the lob swing and play it the same as you would a bunker shot. Take the sand wedge or third wedge, open it up and hit down and through the grass at a point an inch or two behind the ball. This should produce the high, soft shot you want.

Probably the most difficult situations for chipping are imposed by hilly lies, and of these the toughest is unquestionably the downhill lie. The ball tends to shoot low and fast off this lie, so this is where you should soften your impact as much as possible. Use the most lofted wedge you carry, and if you're playing to a downward-sloping green, address the ball with a slightly open face.

At address, try to align your body parallel to the hill, and slant your left toe more towards the hole than usual. That will help prevent you from tilting down the hill during the swing. Play the ball just behind its normal position in your stance, and try to keep your wrists out of this stroke. The key here is to stay with the shot and not quit on it. You need to hit down and through this ball, difficult as that is with the downhill lie.

One strategic consideration: always leave the pin in the hole when you're chipping downhill. The far lip will be lower than the near one, so even a slightly firm shot will tend to roll across the top of the hole. With the flagstick in, you'll give yourself a margin of error.

When I'm chipping uphill, on the other hand, I usually take the pin out. In this case, the back lip is higher and acts almost like a backboard, allowing for a more aggressive stroke. If my lie is uphill, I'll also make a couple of adjustments.

Ball above feet: grip down a bit, and compensate for the tendency to pull the ball by aiming to the right.

First, I'll take a less lofted club than I would for a level-lie chip in the same situation. A 7- or 8-iron, for instance, instead of a 9 or wedge. The tendency from this lie is to leave the chip short, so the straighter-faced club will add some distance.

Again, align yourself with the slope, and flare that left foot towards the target to brace yourself both at address and during the forward swing. Take the club back down along the slope and bring it up through the same path. And since the common error is to be short, think 'sink' and be more aggressive than ever.

When you have a sidehill lie, take a little extra time to plan the shot, because you usually have to allow for the slope. If the ball is above your feet choke down a bit on the club, and aim a bit to the right, to allow for the tendency to pull this shot. From a lie where the ball is below your feet, beware of the dreaded shank. To avoid it, widen your stance a hair, bend over from the waist a bit more

Ball below feet: flex knees, widen stance, and bend over more than usual, and keep most of your weight on your heels.

than normal, and keep your weight back on your heels. And since you'll have a tendency to push a shot from this lie, aim a bit to the left of your target.

The trickiest situation is when you have to deal with a hill that intervenes between your ball and the green. In this situation, the best solution is a bump shot, where you smack the ball into the side of the hill, then let it bounce up and on to the green.

There are a couple of different ways to play it. You can hit a hard shot into the top of the bank and

The bellied wedge: use your putting technique, and glide the leading edge of the sand wedge through the fringe grass and into the back of the ball.

The intentional fat shot: carve into the turf just behind the ball, and the shot will behave much the same way as an explosion from sand.

play it to take one high bounce on to the green, or you can go for more of a skittering shot, with two or three bounces along thc bank. The best way to make your decision is to take a good look at the grass on the hill. If it's long and thick, go for one bounce at the top. If it's short and firm, you can go for the two-bouncer. In either case, take a low-lofted chipper such as a 7- or 8-iron. First determine where you want the ball to land on the green, then ask yourself where you'll have to hit the bank in order to make it pop up on to that landing spot on the green. Since in effect you have two landing spots here, this shot takes more planning than any other.

The shot called for is a sort of punched chip, so play the ball well back, make a short, stiff-wristed swing, and sock into the back of the ball. Then hope that your calculations were accurate.

Finally, here's the shortest of chip shots. In fact, although this shot is played from off the green, it's more like a putt than a chip.

The situation has your ball at the back edge of the fringe, resting against the first cut off rough grass. You can't get a putter through the grass to putt it, and yet a conventional chip shot would be a risk. The solution is to hit the bellied wedge shot. You actually putt the ball with the leading edge of your sand wedge. The heavy flange of the sand wedge will glide smoothly through the long grass and bump the back of the ball just as nicely as a putter.

This may sound like a tough shot, but you'll find after a couple of practice attempts that it comes off very easily. Just use your usual putting grip, stance and swing, being sure to grip down on the shaft of the wedge so that it in effect becomes the same length club as your putter. A stiff-wristed motion works best on this, but the main point is to glide the club smoothly back and through the ball. Practice will tell you that, because the wedge's clubhead is heavier than that of a putter, you don't have to hit this ball as hard as a putt of the same distance.

I Dare You

Hit It Fat

You've seen this situation often. You're off to the side of the green, a bunker between you and the pin, and your ball is sitting down in the rough. You know that, in order to get that ball out of its grave, you'll have to swing so hard that it will soar over the green. It seems you have no shot. But you do.

The right way to play this is with a 'mistake' that every weekend golfer has hit dozens of times – a fat shot. Play it the same way you would a bunker explosion. Widen and open your stance, open your sand wedge so that it points twenty or thirty yards to the right of your target and lay it back so that its face is almost parallel to the ground. Play the ball off your left instep so that your hands are behind the ball.

What you actually want to do on this shot is slice into the turf with the heel of the wedge leading the way. This will open a slit in the ground, and the rest of the club will carve in under the ball. So just pick the club up quickly with your wrists and slug down hard, about an inch and a half behind the ball. You'll strike the ground hard but the ball will come out slower and land softer than any shot you've ever hit. By the way, two things are required in order to play this shot successfully: fairly soft turf and fairly hard practice.

CHAPTER 9

Opportunities

HOW TO MAKE YOUR BEST SHOTS FROM YOUR WORST LIES

I like trouble. In a perverse way, I actually enjoy finding my ball in a bad lie or a tough situation.

Trouble forces me to stretch my shotmaking skills, and that's part of the fun of playing aggressive golf. Besides, when I'm in a tough spot in a tournament, it's sort of fun to have the spectators gather round and speculate on how I'm going to escape. Sometimes I'll kid around with them. If I'm in the trees I'll ask if anyone has a chain saw handy, or something corny like that. Then if I play the shot successfully, they all go crazy and I get a big kick out of it too. The fact is – for the fan or the player – there's no greater thrill in golf than a spectacular recovery shot.

The other reason I like trouble is that it gives me a chance to do something big – to turn the tide of a hole, to convert an apparent bogey or double bogey into a par or birdie. That type of swing can yield tremendous dividends both in one's score and in one's psyche.

Throughout this book I've tried to stress an important theme regarding what it takes to play good golf: attitude is more important than aptitude. If you take the correct mental approach towards the game, the physical capability usually follows. Nowhere is that more important than with regard to trouble play. So try to view bad lies and tough situations as I do – not as setbacks but as opportunities. If that sounds like a tough assignment, the following pages should help.

The Basics

Before you can become a good trouble player you have to become a good trouble thinker. That requires three qualities.

The first is patience. When your golf ball plops into water or deep rough or sails into the centre of the woods, take a deep breath. Then forget that shot and start concentrating on the next one. I get angry sometimes, too, but I've learned that in golf you can't channel such anger towards anything positive. I've also seen lots of players turn their anger into all sorts of negatives.

Some get despondent. They act as if they've been victimised and there's nothing they can do about it. So they give up. When they reach the ball, they take no time or care, they just swipe at it once – sometimes twice or three times. If they don't get it back into play, they close the book on that hole. Sometimes such a predicament will ruin these people for the rest of the day.

Others get angry. They suddenly start to see the golf course as a mortal enemy. They no longer want to hit the ball, they want to hurt it. When this type of player knocks his drive out of bounds and tees up a second ball, he usually hits that second ball into trouble too. Anger blurs his ability to concentrate sharply and swing smoothly.

And still others get overly ambitious. They sense that after their bad shot they've lost a certain amount of ground, and they become determined to regain all of that ground on the next shot. From a thick lie in the centre of a dense forest, this player will take out his 3-wood and go for the flag. That's usually the beginning of a very big number.

If you can keep your cool after hitting a ball into trouble, you'll have a big advantage over all these other types of players (three groups which, from my observation, encompass about 90 per cent of amateur golfers). So whatever it takes, cool yourself down, put the bad shot behind you and repeat to yourself 'Patience, patience.' Later on, you'll be glad you did.

The second quality, which goes hand in hand with patience, is realism. It's important to be able to accept your fate and deal with it. Walter Hagen, the man who won four consecutive PGA Championships, once said that in a given round of golf he expected to miss at least five shots. That way, when his ball rolled into trouble, he was mentally prepared to deal with it. (Hagen, incidentally, was probably the greatest trouble player of all time.)

Be realistic about your next shot as well. Take a businesslike approach to the problem. You hit the ball in there, and you now have to hit it out. Your assignment is to evaluate the various options and choose the shot where reward most outweighs risk. When your ball is 200 yards from a water-guarded green and sitting in eight-inch rough, the shot with the biggest reward may be a 5-wood, but from a poor lie, you'll risk smothering or pulling that shot, or hitting it into the drink. The risks are greater than the reward. An 8-iron layup won't reward you to the same degree, but the risks will be minimal.

The final quality for good trouble play is imagination. You have to be able to 'see' all the shots, all the options available to you. Sometimes this is just a matter of keeping your wits about you and scanning the area for escape routes. I'll never forget the situation I found myself in at Winged Foot in the 1984 US Open.

It was the final hole of the second round, and I had hooked my teeshot into big trouble in the rough of that long par-four. Bob Rosburg was following our group for ESPN at the time, and when he got to my ball, he made one of those dire pronouncements for which he is famous.

'Greg's absolutely dead,' he said. 'He has a solid wall of trees between him and the green, and there's no way through them. His only option is to chip out to the fairway.'

When I got to the ball, I must admit, it didn't look promising. But when among trees I'm a strong believer in looking straight up, in search of a high way out. Sure enough, there was an opening up there. It was only four feet wide, but it was at the exact height for the path of my 6-iron, and a 6-iron was the club I needed to reach that 18th green.

Charlie Earp, my first golf instructor and good friend from Australia, was caddieing for me that week, and when I started peering up into the branches I could see him cringe. But I took out the 6-iron and told him, 'I can get it through there.'

And I did. The ball sailed straight through the centre of that four-foot opening, landed on the green and finished five feet from the hole. Rosburg couldn't believe it.

Actually, the shot itself was nothing fancy, just a solid, straight 6-iron. But hitting the shot wasn't the tough part – *seeing* it was.

As I said, trouble makes me stretch my shotmaking skills, and a good portion of those skills are mental, not physical. I suspect this is true of most touring professional golfers. When we're in a difficult spot, we work harder, concentrate harder. And, more often than not, we pull off the shot.

You may not have the physical skills of a pro, but there's no reason why you can't approach and evaluate trouble situations with the same set of mental acuity. In fact, to use these skills you need nothing more than a sophisticated version of your normal pre-shot routine.

I begin playing a trouble shot as I'm approaching the ball. Often you can see your situation better – get a view of the big picture – when you're a hundred yards behind it. You can see the actual height of the trees, the nature of the terrain the shot will have to cross, and sometimes you can get a better view of the pin position as well.

Once I'm at the ball, the first thing I do is inspect the lie. If it's in heavy grass, several shots are immediately made impossible. Likewise, if it's sitting on hardpan or some other tight lie, certain shots are eliminated. I also make note of whether the grass is wet or dry and whether it's growing with my shot or against it.

Next I take a look at what's in front of me. Let's say I'm in the rough, I have 150 yards to the green and I have to hit the ball under a tree limb that's hanging about six feet off the ground. I begin to imagine what the ideal escape would look like – some sort of punch that lands in the fairway and runs to the green. This is when I start asking myself questions. Does my lie allow me to put the club on the ball for such a shot? (If the grass is very thick, the answer is no.) Can I find my way to the green with such a shot or does a bunker or water hazard block the way?

If the answers to those questions raise doubts about my first shot, I'll search for other options. This is when I look up into the trees for a possible high-road escape. I'll also consider whether a hook or slice would be possible from the situation. If no other option is available, I'll return to the question of the low shot, and make my decision, either to go for the green or to lay up.

Once that choice is made, I'll match a club to the situation. In the case of the shot I've described, let's say I choose to go for the green. I'll next visualise the ideal shot once again, and that picture will automatically tell me the best club to choose, probably a 4- or 5-iron, which I would play back in my stance and hit with a short, crisp, punching swing.

If I make the more difficult decision – to lay up – I'll again imagine what the ideal shot would be. (This is something that amateurs often fail to do. Instead they take a careless, cavalier attitude towards safe shots, and often chip the ball too short or clear across the fairway into further trouble.) I'll decide the ideal point from which I'd like to play my next shot, then I'll visualise hitting my safe shot to that point. Finally, I'll choose the club that offers the best chance of executing that safe shot.

Adopt this type of routine and you'll be pleased with the results. You'll discover, just as the pros do, that the tighter the spot you're in, the tighter your focus of concentration will be, and the more impressive your shotmaking will be.

The Aggressor's Edge

Of course, it's one thing to be able to see the right shot, and quite another to be able to hit the right shot *right*. Earlier chapters have explained how to manoeuvre the ball and how to cope with rough and bunkers, but we've left several corners of the golf course untouched, and it's time to visit them now. Although you may deal with these lies and situations only once in a round, that one shot may be the most pivotal and important one you face all day.

Hills

The most common type of trouble can occur smack in the middle of the fairway – when you're hitting off a hill. There are four basic types of hilly lies – uphill, downhill, sidehill with the ball above your feet, and sidehill with the ball below – and each of these takes some adaptation.

When you have an uphill lie, the first thing to do is take one club more than you normally would. You'll tend to hit the ball a bit higher than normal from this lie, so unless you have a tailwind you'll have to counteract that extra height with a longer-hitting club.

At address, the most important point is to set yourself parallel to the slope. Be sure that your hips and shoulders are on roughly the same incline as the hill. If this means putting a little extra bend in your left knee, do so. The ball should be positioned an inch or so forward of its usual position in your stance, and your weight should be shaded a bit to your left side.

From this set-up swing normally, but in a compact way. If you take too big a swing from this lie, you can make the same mistake I made back on the final hole of the Masters in 1986, when on my backswing I transferred too much weight to my right side and lost balance, falling slightly down the hill. That was the error which caused me to push the ball to the right, leading to a fatal bogey.

So swing smoothly and compactly – don't try to help the ball up – and if you've selected the right club, you'll have no trouble. One final thought – there's a tendency to pull the ball from this lie, so compensate by aiming a few feet right of where you want to go.

From a downhill lie, as you might imagine, everything is just the opposite. Align your body as

Ball above feet: put extra weight on your toes and make a controlled, unhurried swing.

close as possible to parallel to the downward slope, by putting extra flex into your right knee. Play the ball back an inch or so in your stance, and take one club less than usual, to compensate for the lower-than-normal flight you'll get. Your weight should be shaded slightly to your right side, and you should aim a bit to the left of your target, since the tendency from this lie is to lose the ball slightly to the right.

On the swing, take the club back straight along the line of the slope and, as with the uphill shot, keep the swing compact. You may have a tendency to fall forward, and 'walk through' this shot after impact, but that's natural. It means only that you've transferred your weight properly on the downswing.

When the ball is on a sidehill lie and above your feet, you'll tend to swing more flatly and hook the ball, so the key from this lie is to aim several yards to the right of your target.

You'll feel crowded on this slope because the ball will be closer to your hands than normal. But resist the temptation to uncrowd yourself by standing farther away from the ball. That will only increase the flatness of your swing. Instead, simply shorten your grip on the club a bit.

There's also a tendency on this shot to fall backwards on your heels during the swing, so at address put some extra weight on your toes. From this position, make a smooth, unhurried swing.

A sidehill lie with the ball below the feet may be the most difficult of all. For one thing, this is a shank lie. When the ball is down the hill from you, it feels farther away than usual and you tend to stand closer to it in order to feel normal at address. That forces you to make a more upright swing, during which you may fall forward. Even if you just tip forward a little, that's enough to bring your club an inch or so outside its normal path so that you hit the ball with the hosel. The result is a shank.

You can lessen this tendency by taking one club longer than you would from a flat lie. This will help you to make a smooth swing and stay in balance. Also, since the tendency is to fade the ball from this lie, a bit of extra club will help. You should also widen your stance a little bit for this shot, to lower your centre of gravity and inhibit unnecessary leg movement. This will also bring your hands a bit closer to the ball.

Since the tendency will be to fall forward on your toes, distribute your weight a bit more towards your heels than normal at address. You should also be sure that you are 'down to the ball' by bending a bit extra from the waist. As with any hilly situation, make a deliberate, compact swing. And be sure to allow for the inevitable left-to-right drift by aiming a couple of yards left of your target.

Many types of trouble can be handled with the same type of swing. For instance, fairway bunkers, hardpan and sandy rough may all be played basically the same as a fairway shot, with one important difference: play the ball back in your stance about two inches. This change will ensure that you'll contact the ball just before the bottom of your swing arc. There will be no chance that you'll fluff it from the sand or bounce up and skull it off hardpan. Once you make that single change, you're ready to tackle these three types of tough lies. The only other advice I'd give you is to make a smooth swing. In all three of these lies, footing and balance can be a problem, so there's no point in making a difficult situation worse by overswinging. A good general rule is to swing three-quarter length on these shots. In the long run, you'll hit the ball just as far as you would with a big swing – because you'll hit it more squarely.

From all of these lies, I often play an intentional fade, by opening my stance a bit at address. The fade swing increases the steepness of my angle of attack on the ball, further ensuring clean contact.

Ball below feet: take one club longer than usual, put your weight on your toes, and keep plenty of flex in your knees throughout the swing.

Traditional instruction says don't play a watery lie unless half the ball is above the surface. I say you can go at it as long as any part of the ball protrudes.

Booby Traps

Walk softly when you discover your ball nestled in a bunch of leaves or pine needles. I learned this lesson the hard way.

Several years ago I was playing a televised 'Battle of the Sexes' match against LPGA pro Beth Daniel. We were all even on the final hole when I knocked my approach shot to the right of the green under some pine trees.

As I approached the ball, I stepped on a stick of wood. That dislodged another piece of wood which moved one of the pine branches. That branch moved another branch, and another, and the chain reaction set my golf ball in motion. The ensuing penalty cost me the match and, as I recall, $15,000.

So be careful when addressing these lies. It's like playing a game of Pick-Up-Stix and, if the ball moves, you lose. On the other hand, it's important, when you're standing on pine needles or leaves, to give yourself the best possible footing, particularly in the wet. So carefully take a wide, firm stance.

If the shot is a long one, you should try to pick the ball out of its nest. Play the ball a bit forward of its normal position in your stance, and make a low, wide takeaway. The swing, like most swings on trouble shots, should be compact and controlled, made mostly with the arms.

If you have a short shot, punch it out. Pull through the ball on the downswing, and don't be afraid to follow through. The flying debris won't affect your shot.

Another sort of booby trap is the lie among tree roots. If you make the wrong move when playing this shot, you could get more than a penalty stroke – you could get a broken wrist. When I see my ball in this situation, the first thing I do is take out a key or a tee and begin probing around. I poke the area just behind and in front of my ball, to be sure no hidden roots are waiting there to snag my club.

If the lie is safe, the best shot is usually a punch. Occasionally, however, you'll have to invent your own shot in this situation because roots will block the path of your normal takeaway. When that happens, just lock your eyes on the ball, and rely on your hand–eye coordination. Take a very short swing and do your best to reroute the club to the back of the ball.

Divots

Without question the most exasperating type of trouble is the divot lie. You hit the ball smack in the middle of the fairway and what do you get? A lie that's worse than anything in the rough.

Maybe the people you play with allow you to roll the ball out of these things, but the people I play with do not. In the hope that you follow the Rules as strictly as I do, here are a couple of tips on handling divots.

Assuming the ball is in the front or centre of the divot, it's not really that tough. Basically, you punch it out. Just play it back in your stance, and make a three-quarter swing, hitting crisply down and through the ball. Expect the ball to shoot out low, and allow for this by taking one club less than you would for a fairway shot of the same distance.

If the ball is in the back of the divot you have an added problem, because it will be sitting about a half-inch lower than the turf that is immediately behind it. In this case you'll probably need to gouge the ball out with a pitching wedge. Position the ball back of centre in your stance and pick the club up sharply on your backswing. Pull down and through hard, and hold on tight. This ball should really squirt out low.

If you find the ball hugging one of the sides of the divot the best tactic is to play a hook or slice. When the ball is on the outside of the divot, I go at it with an in-to-out swing, taking that outside divot wall out of play. Conversely, when the ball's leaning against the near wall of the divot, I'll cut across it with an out-to-in swing. Of course, in either of these cases, you should allow for some sideward drift on the shot.

Water Blasts

Everyone thinks that an explosion from water is the most daring shot in golf. The reality is, it's no more difficult than a sand blast. The trick is not in knowing how to play it, it's knowing *when* to play it.

I've practised this shot a lot, and I can tell you that when any part of your ball protrudes above the surface of the water, you can safely give it a whack.

Many players and teachers will advise you to hit this shot with a pitching wedge, but I prefer a sand wedge, so I guess either will do. Assuming you have good footing, just play it as you would an explosion from sand, with the ball well back in your open stance. However, be sure to keep your clubface square to your target, to facilitate slicing through the water. Figure on having to hit this shot about twice as hard as you would a fairway shot of the same distance. Also figure on getting soaked.

Trees

Basically, there are four ways of getting out of the trees – by going over them, under them, around to the right or around to the left.

The nature of your lie will disallow various of these options and dictate others. For instance, if you're in heavy grass, you won't be able to put much sidespin on the ball, so you can forget about hooking or slicing around the tree. You'll also have trouble hitting a low shot, because in order to get the ball airborne at all you'll have to go at it with a steep swing. Thus your best bet from rough is usually a high shot. That's one of the reasons I always look upwards when I'm in tree trouble.

If, on the other hand, you're sitting on hardpan or any type of tight lie, the high road is a hazardous one. A low shot or a slice is often the best route out of this situation.

Of course, occasionally you'll find yourself in a predicament where none of the traditional escapes will work. Let's say you're in the final hole of a dead-even match. Your opponent has just played his approach to within birdie range, and you're stymied by a big tree. In this situation you have only one option – you must hit *through* the tree.

It's a desperate shot, to be sure, but if you analyse and approach it intelligently, you'll maximise your chances of pulling it off. First, don't just slug the ball indiscriminately at the tree. Look for the most sparsely foliated area of the tree and then fit your shot to that. The distance to the green may be 150 yards, but you may have to hit anything from an 8-iron to a 2-iron to make the shot work.

Secondly, take at least one club more than you think you need. This will allow the branches to slow the ball's flight a bit. After all, a tree may be 90 per cent air, but so is a screen door, so expect some resistance along the way.

Finally, once you have the ideal shot in mind, take a clear mental picture of it. Visualise your ball shooting through that opening in the tree, and keep that image sharp in your mind as you make your swing. You'll be surprised at how this positive mental picture will help you out of the most negative situations.

Windy Weather

When the wind blows, patience is the key. Realise that you're going to make some mistakes. Realise that every other player will falter as well. Realise that you'll lose distance, lose accuracy, probably lose golf balls too.

In nearly two decades of playing golf all over the world, I've never met a tougher opponent than Mother Nature. I'll never forget the experience I had as an assistant professional at the La Paruse Golf Club in Australia. The wind must have been blowing 50 miles per hour when I got to the tee of the 5th hole, a par-five that plays over the top of a huge hill, and on that day played straight into the teeth of the wind. After a drive to the base of the hill, I took a 5-iron to play over the top.

I hit it well and the ball sailed skywards, climbing with the slope of the hill. But when it got to the top, it just kept climbing, straight up, and then, incredibly, it began to blow backwards. I just stood there gaping as that ball blew all the way back behind me!

Unless you're very unlucky, you'll never experience that type of distance loss in the wind, but you should be prepared to sacrifice some yardage.

Hitting a teeshot into a headwind is one of the most difficult assignments in the game. Traditional advice claims that you should tee the ball lower to hit a more boring shot. I agree with that only for the type of player who sweeps the ball. For a downward-hitting player, the lower tee only encourages an even steeper attack which will result in a high shot that will be battered by the wind. So this player should tee the ball as usual and try to make a long, low, sweeping takeaway.

With a tailwind, of course, you'll get extra distance. Sweeping swingers should tee it a bit higher to get it up in the wind, and downward hitters should position the ball a bit more forward in the stance. No matter which swing you have, you should resist the temptation to wallop the ball. Just swing smoothly – the tailwind will wallop it for you.

On approach shots, I try to keep the ball low in both headwinds and tailwinds, to maximise control of the shot. I widen my stance a bit, play the ball back an inch or so, and make a slightly slower, more compact swing. That's the general strategy I think everyone should follow.

With crosswinds, you should gear your strategy to your level of skill. If you're basically a straight hitter of the ball, with no drift to your shots, playing a crosswind is as simple as aiming to the right or left to allow for the pull of the breeze. If you're a habitual fader/slicer, you'll want to 'ride' the left-to-right winds for maximum distance and 'fight' the right-to-left winds for maximum accuracy. The opposite is true for someone who usually hits a draw or hook. Of course, if you are sufficiently accomplished to work the ball with confidence in either direction, then you ride the crosswinds on your teeshots and fight them on your approaches.

Rainy Weather

I guess the worst weather conditions I've ever seen were during a Bing Crosby Pro–Am a few years ago. With three holes to go in the second round I was within one stroke of the lead, and believe it or

The lefty shot: turn a 9-iron on its toe, reverse your grip positions, and make a compact swing.

not, I missed the cut. Facing the 16th, 17th and 18th holes at Cypress Point, and playing in a howling, soaking gale, I finished triple-bogey six, quintuple-bogey nine, double-bogey six!

That day, my only objective was to get to the clubhouse alive. In most rainy conditions, however, the aim is more simple – keep yourself and your equipment as dry as possible. We professionals have an edge in this regard. With huge golf bags and caddies to carry them for us, we can load up with all sorts of apparel and equipment to shelter us from the wet stuff. On a rainy tournament day, I'll take an umbrella, a complete rainsuit, five or six towels, plus at least ten gloves.

And on some days I've used all ten of those gloves. Indeed if there's one part of your body to keep dry it's your hands. Once you lose your grip, you lose everything. So keep your hands in your pockets except to play. Also, be sure to keep the top of your golf bag covered so that rain doesn't drip

The one-handed chop: with your back towards the target, grip the 9-iron with your right hand only. After a couple of practice swings, hit the ball with a wristy chop.

down the shafts and get your grips wet. If all else fails you can improve your hold on the club by wrapping a handkerchief around the grip. (Yes, it's within the Rules.)

Since the club always slips in wet weather, your main swing key is to hold on tight. Other than that, be sure to give yourself good footing, particularly on the teeshot. Because of your tight grip, you'll have less of a free-flowing swing, so you can expect less distance on your drives. Likewise on the

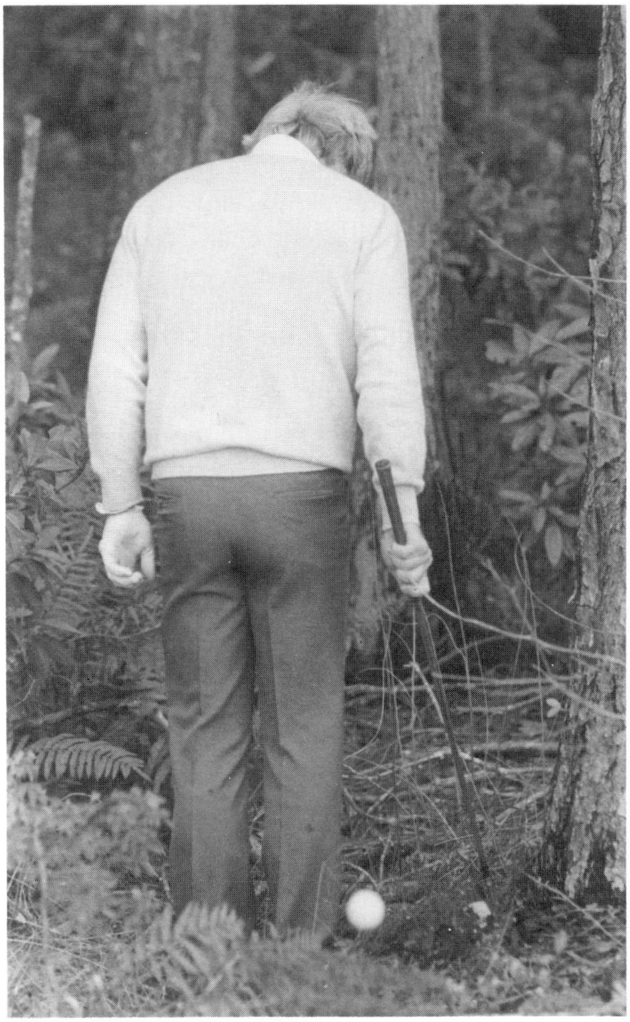

second shots where the soggy turf swallows up your club and impedes solid impact. So allow yourself at least one club more on approaches.

One advantage of playing in wet weather is that the greens will be soft, so you'll be able to fire your shots right at the flag. And if the greens should begin to form puddles, you should hit your short irons and pitches right at the puddles that are close to the hole, because they'll stop the ball dead. You may then drop to the nearest spot that affords you a dry line to the cup. And be sure to give your putts an extra measure of firmness, because a wet green is always a slow one.

The Best Kind of Experience

The best way to develop a scrambling ability is to gain some experience, and the best way to get that experience is not in actual play but in practice. So the next time you're headed for the driving range, go instead to a quiet area of the golf course. Toss some balls into the woods, and then go find them and play them out – take whatever the lie gives you and do your best with it. If some lies don't permit you to make bold recovery shots, then play the balls out safe. That shot takes some practice too.

Then give yourself some lies in divots, in leaves and needles, on hardpan and hills, and even one or two in water. See how the ball reacts from these positions, and watch how the prescribed adjustments in stance and swing produce the escapes you need. A couple of sessions like this will give you the ability and confidence you need to handle whatever the gods of golf throw your way.

I Dare You

Three Trick Shots

I hate taking unplayable lies, and you should too. It's like an admission of defeat. The following three shots are for those situations that seem unplayable but are not. They just require a little ingenuity.

The first shot is played when your ball lies so

The kneeling shot: aim well to the right of your target, lock your eyes on the ball, and make a short, stiff-wristed scrape at the ball, almost like a putt.

close to an obstacle that you can't take a stance or swing from the conventional side. So you play it left-handed.

If the ball is sitting cleanly, the best club to use is a putter, if you have one of those models that may be hit either right or left handed. Failing this, take a 9-iron, and turn the club so that the blade stands on its toe. Grip it like a lefty, with your left hand below your right on the club.

Try a couple of practice swings to get the feel of this shot. Then address the ball with the toe of the club, and make a short, crisp swing. The ball may go several yards, it may go only a few feet, but in either case you should be better off than if you were to take an unplayable lie.

The second shot is an alternative to the lefty shot, when you need a bit more distance. I call it the one-handed chop. Take the same 9-iron, grip it with only your right hand, and stand with your back towards your target. The ball should be positioned about nine inches diagonally in front and to the right of your right toe.

From this position the swing is nothing more than a wristy chop. Again, make a couple of practice chops before you try the real thing. If you hit this one squarely, you can move the ball fifty yards or more.

Finally, when your ball comes to rest under a low-lying tree or bush, try the kneeling shot. If you follow the US PGA Tour, you'll recall the controversy when Craig Stadler played this shot in the 1987 San Diego Open. Stadler spread a towel on the ground and knelt on it to protect his slacks, unaware that a recent USGA decision had deemed such a practice to be a way of building a stance, and thus a breach of the Rules. A day after Stadler committed the foul, a TV viewer who saw a tape of the shot reported the infraction. Stadler was penalised, and because he had failed to assess himself the penalty, was disqualified for signing an invalid scorecard.

So if you decide to play this shot, kneel on the ground and on nothing else. (My demonstration in the photos here is just that, a demonstration, so I too am kneeling on a towel. If this were the real thing, rest assured, the towel would be absent!) Take a wedge or 9-iron and align yourself well to the right of where you want to go. With your arms at shoulder height you'll be making a very flat swing, and with the loft on of the club actually pointing to the left, you'll have to compensate.

Once you're aligned, lock your eyes on the ball and make a short, stiff-wristed swing – almost like a big putt. You'll be surprised at how well you can recover, even after the course has brought you to your knees.

CHAPTER 10

Be Greedy on the Green

WHY I PUTT BOLDLY AND YOU SHOULD TOO

Earlier in this book I advised you to play as aggressively as you feel on each particular day. But actually that advice applies only to the long game. Once you're on the green, you should try to do the same thing every day, on every putt – ram it into the back of the hole.

Hubert Green, whose game and record I respect greatly, has a different philosophy of putting from mine. He says his object is to leave the ball in the best place for his next putt. That may sound strategic, but to me it's simply negative thinking. If you entertain the possibility of a 'next' putt, you're not focusing on sinking the one you have.

You'll note that I'm rarely short with my putts, whether they're hit from sixty feet or six feet. I frankly don't care where I leave the ball because if for some reason I don't sink my first putt, I'm absolutely confident I'll sink the next one, no matter where I leave it. Indeed, no matter where on the green, where in the tournament I stand, I have but one goal when I stand over a putt – to sink it.

The Basics

As important as this bold, aggressive stroke is to my game, it's even more important to yours. In fact, I can think of ten good reasons why every amateur golfer should putt aggressively.

1. *You'll improve your chances.* There are only four ways to miss a putt – by hitting it too far to the left, too far to the right, too long or too short. However, if you strike all of your putts firmly to the hole, you'll immediately eliminate one of those four ways. Besides, as the old golf saying goes 'Never up, never in.'

2. *Statistics have proved, bold is best.* Dave Pelz, the man nicknamed 'Professor Putt' because of the voluminous research he has done on all aspects of putting, has proved that the ideal putt is a firm one. Using a special putting robot, Pelz hit thousands of putts and showed that the putt that has the best chance of dropping is one that is struck with sufficient force to take the ball seventeen inches *past the hole*.

3. *A firm stroke is a good stroke.* A bold putter always hits the ball with an accelerating motion through impact, and a steady, smooth, accelerating stroke is one of the marks of all proficient, confident putters.

4. *The psychological factor.* Think back on the last time you missed several putts in a row by leaving them short. Pretty mad at yourself, weren't you? Chronic shortness can unravel even the best players. But if you miss a few putts by hitting them *past* the hole, the effect is rarely as severe. At least you know that you gave them all a chance.

5. *A bold stroke travels best.* Some greens are better conditioned than others. A lagging type of stroke may work fine on smooth, fast greens, where you can gently roll the ball to the hole. On coarse, bumpy greens, however, lagging rarely works. The aggressive method, on the other hand, is equally suited to any green and it can give you a big edge when you're competing on shaggy surfaces.

6. *Bold is best on long putts.* If you go past the hole on your approach putt, you can watch how the ball behaves near the cup. For instance, when the ball tails off from left to right, you can be pretty certain that your return putt will break from right to left. If you leave an approach putt short of the hole, however, you have no 'experience' near the cup, and the speed and break of your second putt will necessarily be something of a guess. That uncertainty can make the hole seem very small.

7. *Bold is best on short putts.* Except on the most severe slopes, if you strike the ball firmly for the back of the cup, you'll be able to aim your two- and three-footers straight at the hole. This takes a lot of the difficulty and worry out of the knee-knockers. Both your confidence and your competence will increase.

8. *Boldness helps you analyse your stroke.* When you get the ball to the cup every time, you can begin to see patterns in your putting. You may have an alignment problem which makes you hit everything to the right. Or there may be a weakness in your stroke which causes you to pull the ball to the left. But if you tend to leave the ball short a lot, you can't observe these things as easily.

9. *Bold is best for match play.* In match play – the format under which most weekend players compete – an aggressive stroke is even more important than for those of us on the pro circuit. Sinking a long putt on the Tour means only that we lower our 72-hole score by one stroke. Sinking a long putt in a match often means winning the hole, sometimes winning the match itself. And it *always* has an unsettling effect on one's opponent.

10. *Bold is best for amateurs.* You may never be able to hit a drive as hard as I do, but there's no reason why you can't putt the ball as hard as I do, and a big reason why you should. After all, you can recover from a short drive with a good iron; you can recover from a short approach with a deft chip. But there's no recovering from a putt that is left short – it's a stroke lost forever. So don't cheat yourself in this area where you have every capability, and at least ten reasons, to be bold and proficient.

When your posture is correct, your hands hang naturally from your shoulders to the grip of the club.

Today, I putt with the same basic method I used when I began playing golf at age fifteen. It seems logical, it's simple, it feels good and it works for me. It always has.

There was a short period of time, however, when I didn't use this method. It began back at the 1978 British Open at St Andrews. I was playing a practice round with my countryman, five-times British Open Champion Peter Thomson, when Peter offered me some advice. He said I'd never become a truly great putter with the open stance and swinging-door stroke I used, and he suggested I develop a square stance and a straight-back/straight-through stroke, in order to ensure keeping the ball dead on line.

It made sense to me, and it seemed easy enough to do. Thus it fulfilled the first two of my basics. Besides, who was I, a young kid fresh on the Tour, to argue with a five-times Open Champion. I gave Thomson's advice a try.

I stand very tall when putting, with my feet close together and my arms stretched straight from my shoulders to the club, almost no bend. My stroke is all arms and shoulders, with the clubface opening slightly on the backswing and closing after impact.

For seven long years I gave it a try. The weakness, I finally realised, was that it didn't satisfy my third basic requirement – I simply wasn't comfortable with the square-to-square technique. In the process of working on it, I tried a half-dozen putters, and never got to the point where I was absolutely confident over the ball.

Ironically, it was at St Andrews again that I abandoned the method and went back to my old style. I'm not sure what prompted me, but one morning during the 1985 Dunhill Cup I simply stuck my old Wilson 8802 putter back in the bag, went to the practice green, and started putting like a kid again. The following year was by far my best as a professional, due in large part to the fact that, statistically, I was the leading putter on the US PGA Tour.

So learn from my mistake. If your putting stance and stroke feel natural and work well, and if you usually get through eighteen holes with thirty

putts or fewer, stick with your method. I don't care whether you putt cross-handed, left-handed, stiff-wristed, floppy-wristed, pigeon-toed, knock-kneed or standing on your head. If your method feels and works fine, keep it.

If, on the other hand, you're uncomfortable with your present putting method, abandon it. I'd never offer this advice so blithely with regard to a full golf swing. But putting is different. It's fundamentally a Machiavellian pursuit – the ends justify the means. So if you don't like the way you're now putting, experiment. Go and try different methods until you come upon a style that feels comfortable, and propels the ball boldly into the hole.

My own stroke feels good to me because I've used it for so many years. I stand very tall, with my feet only an inch or so apart and my arms stretched straight down from my shoulders with almost no bend. This gives me a feeling of unity with the putter shaft.

I also stand open just a hair. Although I'm sure I did this originally simply because it felt comfortable, I can now say that it gives me a slightly better look at the hole than I had with the square stance.

I use a reverse overlap grip – the index finger of my left hand overlapping the little finger of my right – to minimise wrist action, and I play the ball in the same position I do for full shots, a hair behind my left heel. This leaves my hands directly over the ball. Again, this feels comfortable, but it also fulfils the other two goals I have for every aspect of my game – it's logical and simple.

My stroke is wristless, generated by my shoulders and arms. As I said earlier, the head of the putter opens slightly on the backswing and closes down after impact, in response to the rotating of my shoulders. I make no attempt to keep the face square throughout the stroke. However, this method does bring the face into a square position through the impact area.

The most distinctive aspect of my putting method is undoubtedly the fact that I address the ball off the toc of my clubface. You'll recall that I do the same thing on full shots. Before taking the club away for a full swing, however, I slide the clubface outwards so that it sits squarely behind the ball. On my putts I begin my backswing from the toe-address position, then reroute the putter during the stroke so that at impact I hit the ball smack off the sweetspot. Again, no explanations for this little wrinkle except that I've done it that way since I was fifteen, and it works.

As with full swings, it's important to have a consistent pre-shot routine, a sort of countdown of things to do before striking the ball. This keeps your mind off negative thoughts and establishes a rhythm for the entire stroke.

On the green that countdown should also encompass the matter of lining up the putt. My routine begins when I align my golf ball, being sure to turn it so that I strike the label. (There's no magic to orienting the ball in this manner – it's simply a way of developing a consistent pattern.)

Next, I begin surveying the putt. First, I look at it from behind the ball towards the hole. Then I double-check, from behind the hole towards the ball. On my way back to the ball, if it's a right-to-left-breaking putt, I'll take a look at it from the left side, vice versa for a left-to-right breaker. By this time, I'll have a good image of the way the ball will run.

Once back at the ball, I'll make two practice strokes, keeping the break and distance of the putt firmly in mind as I do so. Then I'll step to the ball, take one final look at the hole, and make my stroke.

The Aggressor's Edge

Stroking the ball is only one part of putting – the mechanical part. Equally important is the artful side – reading the green.

Good green reading comes with experience. After hitting enough putts over enough different types of terrain and grass, you develop a sixth sense of how the ball will roll. As you walk on to a green, whether you realise it or not, you take in all sorts of subtle information.

If the green appears light, you know you're putting against the grain; if it's dark you're downgrain. If the green is set on a high area of the course and you feel a breeze as you step on to it, you sense that the putt will be fast. Even if you don't look closely at the surrounding terrain, you are aware of any major slope in the land. Without having to tell

The most distinctive aspect of my putting method is that I address putts off the toe of my putter yet hit them off the sweet spot.

My putting routine begins when I set my ball down, always aligning it the same way.

yourself, you know which is the low side of the green and which is the high. If the putting surface is hard and crusty under foot, you receive one message, if it's soft and spongy you get another. Experience with many, many putts allows you to run these data through your computer before you even mark your ball.

The most elusive aspect of green-reading has to do with the grain. 'Grain' refers to the direction in which the blades of grass grow. The light/dark appearance is one way to read it. Another method you can use is to take your putter blade and scrape it across a patch of fringe. If the blades of grass brush up, you're scraping against the grain. If they mat down, you're scraping with it. (Incidentally, be sure to do this scraping on the fringe; on the greens, it's against Rule 35-1f.) A third method is to take a look at the cup. Often, the blades of grass will grow over the edge of the cup in the direction in which the grain moves. Incidentally, grain usually grows towards water, especially towards the ocean, and in the east it's apt to lean towards the mountains. If you're not near any such geography, figure on the grain growing in the direction of the setting sun.

Grain is strongest on bermuda grass, where the

short crewcut-like blades tend to push the ball strongly. Although each putt on each green is different, as a general rule you can figure on stroking the ball about 20 per cent harder than usual on a putt that's dead into the grain, and about 20 per cent less on a downgrain putt. When the ball breaks with the grain, read in extra 'borrow' on the putt. When the slope is against the grain, play for less break. These effects are less marked on the long-stemmed bent and other strains of grass, but they are present nonetheless.

The break of your putt will also be affected by the firmness of a green, the wetness/dryness, the amount of wind you're facing, and even the time of day. In general, any time you have to hit the ball hard, you play for less break.

My first inspection of the break is from behind the ball looking at the hole.

Next I'll walk around and look back through the hole to the ball.

On a right-to-left putt, I check the slope from the left side; on a left-to-right putt, I'll look at it from the right.

CONDITIONS

Play more break	*Play less break*
1. Hard green	1. Soft green
2. Dry green	2. Wet green
3. Grain with slope	3. Grain against slope
4. Downhill	4. Uphill
5. Bermuda grass, kikuyu	5. Bent grass, rye
6. Afternoon	6. Morning
7. Crosswind with slope	7. Crosswind against slope
8. Light tailwind	8. Headwind, heavy tailwind

The putt that has the best chance of dropping is one that is struck with enough force to take it seventeen inches past the hole.

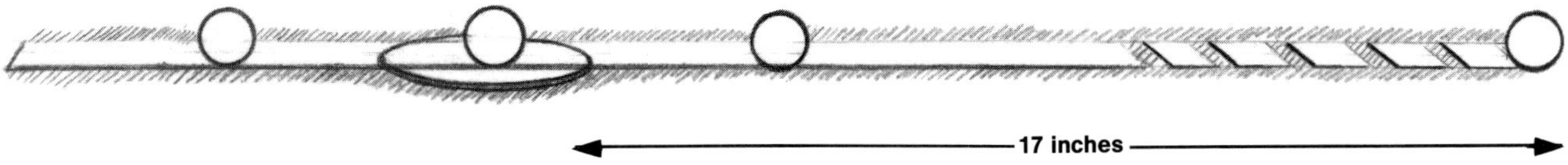

Another way of reading the break on a green is to watch the way other players' putts behave. I'm all for this 'going to school', but with one caveat: allow for any difference between your own playing style and those of your fellow players. If, for instance, your friend is a lagger and you're a charger, don't play as much break as he does.

Finally, if I have one hard and fast rule in putting, it's this: never hit the ball until you have a good vision of the path on which it will roll. Sometimes – we all know those golden moments – the vision will come to you immediately. You'll 'see' the perfect putt the minute you step up to it and, more often than not, you'll sink it just as you saw it. Other times, it will take much longer to get a picture of the putt, and even then you won't be comfortable. But don't make your stroke until you have the best read you can get. You have to believe in your line if you want to have a good chance of sinking any putt.

When the putt has lots of break in it, be sure to visualise the entire path that the ball will take, particularly the last part as it drops. And if it must come in from one side, visualise that moment in particular. Keep in mind that every cup has sort of a gate or doorway. On straight putts the doorway faces directly parallel to the blade of your putter. On putts that break, however, you must mentally re-position that doorway – slide it clockwise or counterclockwise around the cup to allow for the sidewinding approach of the ball.

I'm a confirmed 'spot putter', which means that once I have the path of the ideal putt visualised, I pick out a point at the crest of the break, and orient my eyes, my putter blade and my mind towards that point rather than at the hole. After all, if my read is correct, and if I hit that spot with the correct speed, the rest of the putt will take care of itself.

This was exactly my thinking on the final green of the 1984 US Open at Winged Foot. After an errant second shot and an indifferent pitch, I faced a forty-foot downhill, sidehill putt for par. I knew I needed to make it if I wanted to have any chance of tying Fuzzy Zoeller, playing directly behind me.

As I lined up that putt, I noticed a small brown spot on the green, about twenty feet in front of my ball and exactly in the path of my ideal putt. 'Okay,' I told myself, 'just get this thing to roll over that spot, and you'll make it.'

It was one of those putts that felt right the moment I struck it. And when I saw it go smack over my spot I knew it was going to be close. Down the hill it curled, and then bam, into the centre of the hole, causing the gallery to erupt and prompting the now-famous 'towel salute' from Fuzzy, who had seen the whole thing from back in the 18th fairway. The next day it was I who returned that gesture of surrender to Fuzzy, after he drubbed me in the eighteen-hole playoff. Still, I'm awfully proud of making that clutch putt on Sunday afternoon.

So search for those spots and discolorations in the green that you can use to discipline your aim on putts. This practice also teaches you to ensure that

When you watch an approach putt go past the cup, you immediately see the way the return putt will break.

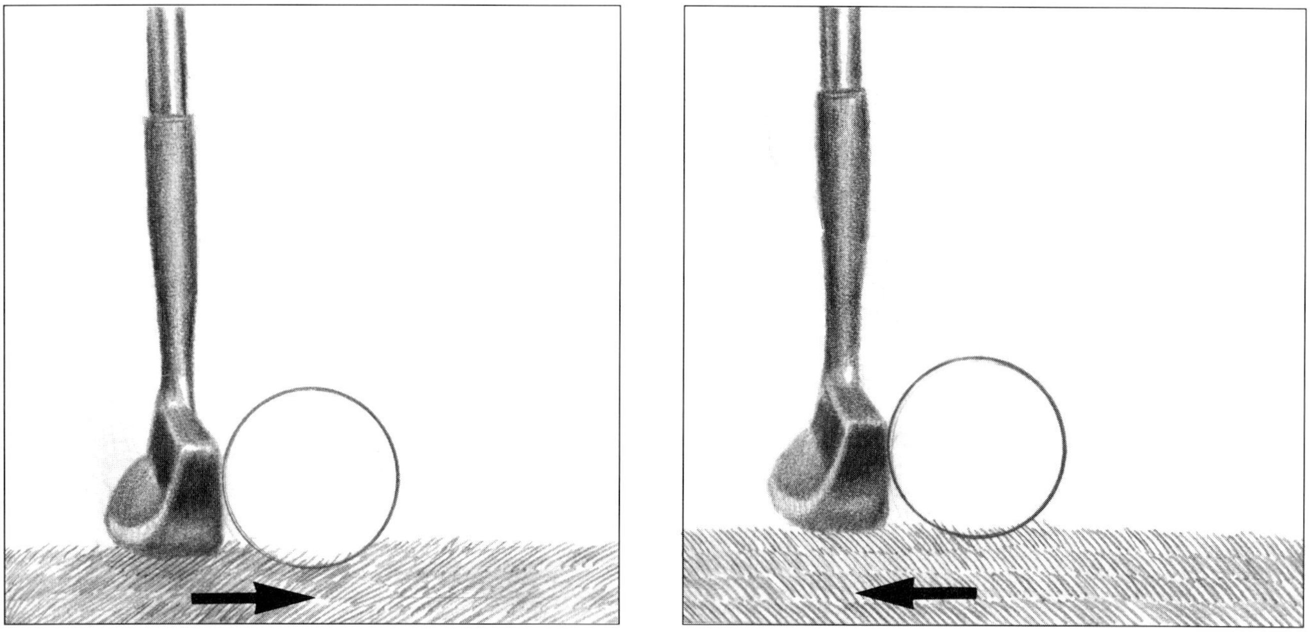

When putting with the grain, stroke the ball about 20 per cent more softly than usual; against the grain, hit it about 20 per cent harder.

the line of your putt is a smooth one, free of twigs, debris and particularly ball marks. (Ball marks, by the way, are a 'hot button' with me. I often repair two or three of them on a green, and I can't understand why every player can't take care of his own. In fact I once went so far as to suggest that players be fined $50 for failing to repair their ball marks.)

Once you have the line in mind, ingrain it by continuing to visualise the ideal path of the putt. Ingrain the feel for distance too, as you take your practice strokes. Don't just flip the putter back and forth – stroke an imaginary ball with exactly the force you plan to impart on your putt. One trick I often use to help me get a better feel for distance is to have my caddie keep the pin in the hole – even on very short putts. People often ask me why I do this, and the reason is that the image of the yellow or white flagstick against the dark rim of the cup is far more vivid than just the hole itself. It's an image that stays in my mind after I've taken my final look

No matter what shot I'm visualising, I concentrate on the apex of the ball's journey. In putting, I pick out a spot at the very crest of the break. Then I orient my eyes, my putter blade and my mind towards that point rather than the hole itself.

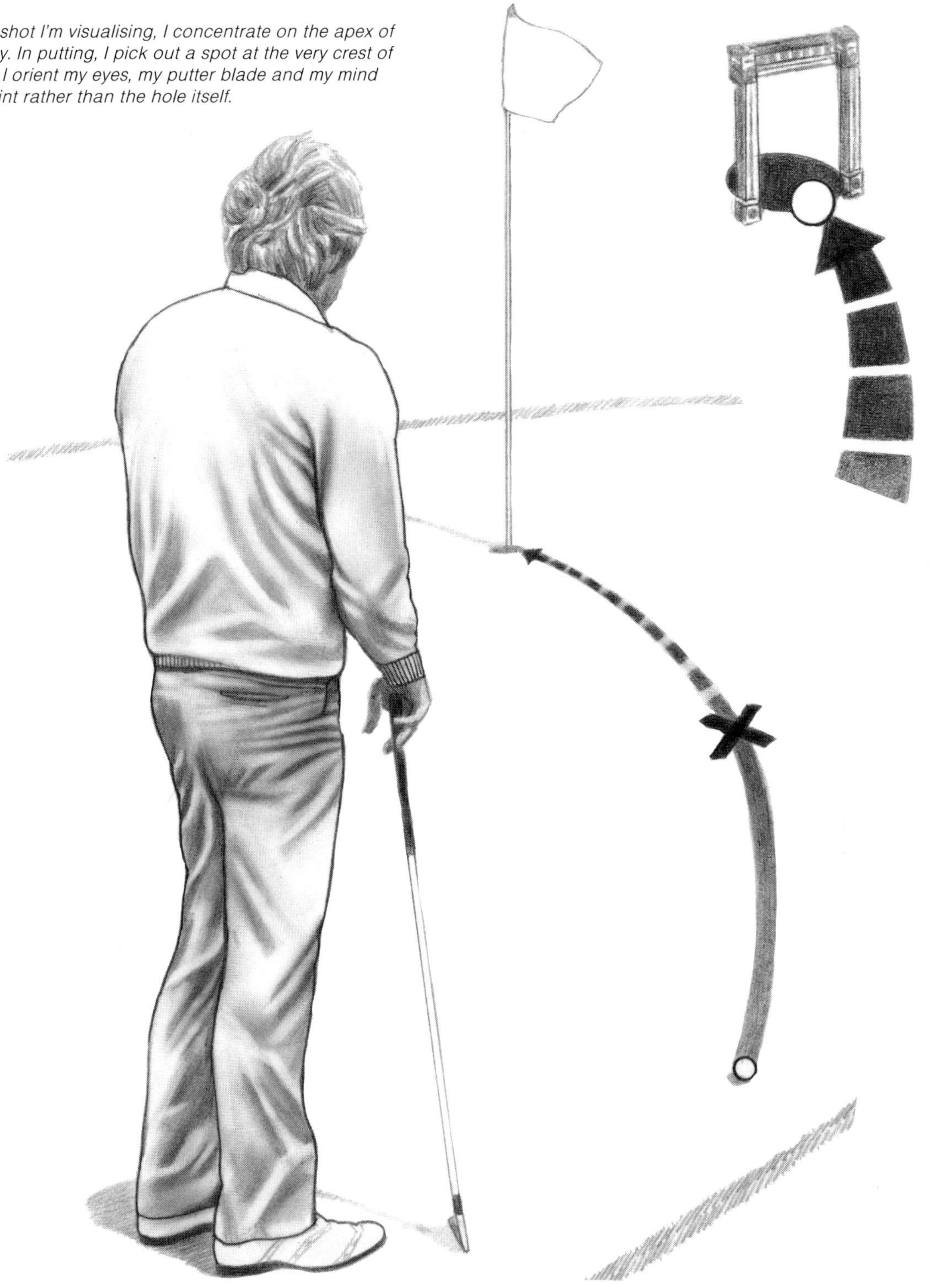

at the hole, and transfers directly to my arms and hands to help me make the proper stroke for the distance I'm facing.

Distance is by far the most important consideration on putts of twenty feet or more. Hit the ball the correct length, and even if you misjudge your direction you'll rarely finish more than a foot or so from the hole. Keep in mind, however, that 'proper length' for an aggressive putter means striking the ball with enough force to rattle it into the cup.

The only way to get a touch for distance is to practise. Someday, spend fifteen minutes hitting the same fifty-foot putt, and at the end of that session you'll be able to hit it consistently within a couple of feet of the hole. It's just a matter of training your hand and arm muscles to respond to what your eye sees, then refining that ability through repetition.

Long-putt practice always gives me sort of a general sense of feel. For more refined touch, I like

A great way to teach both of your hands their role in the putting stroke, and to develop feel, is to hit practice putts with each hand individually.

For the ultimate test of your concentration, your stamina and your nerves, try sinking twenty-five three-footers in a row. Once you have achieved that, move up to four-footers.

to work on the fast downhillers, particularly those with some break in them. This is without question the hardest type of putt. Usually, I'll hit it off the toe of the putter; this deadens the hit a bit while still allowing me to make a normal stroke.

I practice uphill putts when I want to work on the mechanics of my stroke. Whereas on a downhiller you simply want to get the ball moving on the proper line with the proper pace, on the uphiller you have to *make* it go. If you want to be successful when putting up a steep slope, you must keep your head down and steady, keep the putter head low going back and accelerate through the ball – all hallmarks of a good stroke.

I Dare You

Sink twenty-five in a row

The last part of my putting practice session is always the short putts – these are the ones I work on to hone not my touch or my stroke but my nerves. I actually play a practice game against myself, to instil some simulated tension. (In truth the tension is far from fake – I get pretty keyed up while playing this game.)

The idea is simple. You try to make twenty-five short putts in a row. Start with two-footers. That may sound easy, but try it. Note when you get to the last few balls, how tense you become. If you have no trouble with the two-footers, go to three-footers. I bet you don't make twenty-five of them in a row on your first try. In fact, you may be there quite a while.

When I have a full-blown putting practice session, I'll hit the three-footers until I make twenty-five of them, then I'll go to four-footers, and work until I make twenty-five of those. Then, assuming it's still light out, I'll try five-footers. Once in a great while, I'll graduate to six-footers. I've only made twenty-five straight six-footers a couple of times in my life. Believe me, on those evenings I left the practice green with a great feeling – and a great sense of feel.

GREG NORMAN – THE FACTS

Open Championship Performances

Year	*Venue*	*Position*	*Scores*	*Total*	*Money*
1977	Turnberry	T–71	78 72 74	224	£200
1978	St Andrews	T–29	72 73 74 72	291	£527
1979	Royal Lytham	T–10	73 71 72 76	292	£4,000
1980	Muirfield	85	74 74 76	224	£350
1981	Royal St George's	T–31	72 75 72 72	291	£875
1982	Royal Troon	T–27	73 75 76 72	296	£1,600
1983	Royal Birkdale	T–19	75 71 70 67	283	£2,957
1984	St Andrews	T–6	67 74 74 67	282	£16,390
1985	Royal St George's	T–16	71 72 71 73	287	£7,900
1986	Turnberry	1	74 63 74 69	280	£70,000
					£104,799

1987 Worldwide Performances

Venue	*Position*	*Scores*	*Total*	*Money*
Tournament of Champions	T–3	69 70 70 71	280	$29,800
Pebble Beach Pro-Am	T–60	72 74 72 75	293	$1,296
Australian Match Play	T–5	Lost quarter-finals		$2,500
Australian Masters	1	68 67 68 70	273	$38,000
Victoria Open	2	66 73 71 68	278	$8,500
Honda Classic	T–5	77 72 67 69	285	$21,900
Bay Hill Classic	T–23	74 70 71 68	283	$5,190
Tournament Players Championship	T–4	67 68 71 70	276	$44,000
Masters Tournament	T–2	73 74 66 72	285	$79,200
Heritage Classic	T–17	72 70 69 66	277	$9,100
Houston Open	T–22	73 72 74 65	284	$5,570
Panasonic Las Vegas Invitational	T–17	71 71 67 70	279	$14,750
Byron Nelson Classic	T–6	64 68 67 70	269	$19,425
Memorial Tournament	T–27	70 72 69 72	283	$6,700
Kemper Open	T–4	64 73 68 73	278	$28,933
US Open	T–51	72 69 74 77	292	$3,462
				$318,326

Provided by: International Management Group

Career Victories (41)

1976	West Lakes Classic
1977	Martini International
	Kusaha Invitational
1978	South Seas Classic
	New South Wales Open
1979	Hong Kong Open
	Martini International
1980	French Open
	Scandinavian Open
	Suntory World Match Play
	Australian Open
1981	Australian Masters
	Martini International
	Dunlop Masters
1982	Dunlop Masters
	State Express Classic
	Benson & Hedges International
1983	Hong Kong Open
	Australian Masters
	Suntory World Match Play
	Kapalua Invitational
	Queensland Open
	New South Wales Open
1984	Kemper Open
	Canadian Open
	Victoria Open
	Australian Masters
	Australian PGA
1985	Australian PGA
	Australian Open
	New South Wales Open
	Dunhill Cup (Australian Team)
1986	Panasonic Las Vegas Invitational
	Kemper Open
	British Open
	Panasonic European Open
	Dunhill Cup (Australian Team)
	Suntory World Match Play
	Queensland Open
	New South Wales Open
	South Australia Open
	Western Australia Open
1987	Australian Masters

Worldwide Earnings

Year	*Rank*	*Total*
1976	—	$17,360
1977	95	$51,225
1978	75	$69,754
1979	59	$97,968
1980	11	$242,874
1981	21	$218,249
1982	23	$226,059
1983	11	$366,819
1984	3	$533,405
1985	15	$392,720
1986	1	$1,146,584
1987	(to date)	$318,326
	Total	US $3,681,343

Sony World Rankings

(and *World of Professional Golf* rankings prior to 1986)

Year	*Rank*
1979	21
1980	13
1981	13
1982	12
1983	4
1984	3
1985	3
1986	1
1987 (to date)	1